RUBY'S Health Quest

...and the answers

from DR ALAN MARYON DAVIS

RUBY'S *Health* Quest

...and the answers

from DR ALAN MARYON DAVIS

Published by **BBC Books,**
an imprint of BBC Worldwide Publishing, BBC Worldwide Limited, Woodlands,
80 Wood Lane, London W12 0TT

First published 1995

ISBN 0 563 37137 4

Designed by **Bobby Birchall, Town Group Consultancy**
Cartoons by **Mark Draisey**
Photographs by **Trevor Leighton**

Printed and bound in Great Britain by Clays Ltd, St Ives plc
Cover printed by Clays Ltd, St Ives plc

Accompanies the series **Ruby's Health Quest**,
made for **BBC TV** by **Prospect Pictures**

About the Author

Alan Maryon Davis is one of this country's best known media doctors, familiar to millions from his many TV and radio interviews and such peak-time series as BBC1's *Bodymatters*, which he co-presented with Dr Grahame Garden and Dr Gillian Rice. He is the agony doctor for *Woman* magazine and the author of eight popular books on health including the best-selling *Diet 2000*. In his spare time he is a public health doctor in south London and a member of the humorous singing group *Instant Sunshine*.

WHEN YOU'RE YOUNG, the word 'health' is as relevant to your life as yak butter. You wake each day assuming that the large mass of meat below your neck will function as well as it did the day before.

Then two things can happen that can shake you to the nub. First, you get sick, or second, you can become aware of...the word makes my flesh crawl... **'STATISTICS'**. From this point on you will arise each day feeling yourself up in the endless hunt for lumps, start checking your own urine, rip the sausage rolls or other fatty foods out of the startled mouths of those around you, and end up spending a fortune on specialists who claim to analyze your nose hairs. This is where the search for well-being can seriously damage your health.

FOREWORD by Ruby Wax

WHAT IS HEALTH?

66 *What is this thing called health?
I mean here I am questing away like
crazy, searching high and low, through
fat and thin, clinic and gym, from
flotation tank to army assault course,
searching for that elusive butterfly,
health. And do you know, the harder
I look, the worse I feel. Come on,
what's the answer?* **99**

Well, I suppose we all have our own idea of what good health is meant to be. Perhaps you picture all those people in the TV adverts: bright eyes, glossy hair, gleaming teeth, bronzed finely-chiselled features, wonderful bodies leaping and bounding with untrammelled glee.

Or perhaps you imagine a life without any pain or suffering. All your bits working in perfect harmony.

Or then again, you might see health as simply being able to manage reasonably comfortably. To get by without too much trouble. Whichever way you regard good health, there's a lot of truth in the old adage: you only really know good health when you've lost it.

 So how can I make sure I don't lose it?

 By looking after yourself and taking a bit of time and trouble to keep yourself in good nick. By watching what you eat. By keeping yourself active. By learning how to cope with stress. By avoiding unhealthy habits. And by knowing what to do if things go wrong.

Q **That's a tall order. Where do I start?**

A Well, I suggest you begin by checking yourself out to see how daunting the challenge is. Just how healthy, or unhealthy, are you? Run yourself through the road-test in the next chapter and find out.

Okay,
let's get going!

CHECK-UP

66 *Paranoia drove me to have many check-ups where I was asked to blow, suck, trot, give blood and spread 'em. What I wanted was a total body scan. Some kind of high-tech, Star Trek, 'barometer thingie' that could give me an accurate print-out of which part of me would give out first and where I could get cheap replacements.* **99**

Yes, I catch your drift. You mean something more than a thermometer – but less than a hospital. Fine, no problem. But I don't think it'll be quite the one-stop, high-tech, ultra-probe you have in mind. In fact, we can make a good start with just a few searching questions, the bathroom scales and the bottom step of the stairs.

The bottom step of the stairs?

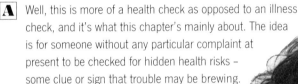 Yes, indeed. We'll get on to that in a moment. But first, just a few words about check-ups in general. They come in two main varieties: those that try to find out the cause of your current problem (if you have one) and those that look for signs of a disease that you might be susceptible to in the future.

The first kind includes all those consultations you might have with your GP, nurse, hospital specialist, dentist, optometrist, pharmacist, therapist or alternative practitioner in an attempt to sort out what's ailing you. It might be anything from a headache to a hernia, from indigestion to impetigo, from gum disease to gall bladder trouble, from acne to asthma, from...

 Okay, okay, I get the idea. What about the second kind of check-up?

 Well, this is more of a health check as opposed to an illness check, and it's what this chapter's mainly about. The idea is for someone without any particular complaint at present to be checked for hidden health risks – some clue or sign that trouble may be brewing.

 Is this the same as health screening?

 Well, screening is certainly one form of check-up, especially if a particular test is involved, like measuring your blood pressure, testing your blood or urine, taking a cervical smear or mammogram (breast X-ray).

But just asking you about your lifestyle: things like eating, drinking, exercise, sleep, stress, smoking, medication, drugs and so on, is an important way of finding out about your health.

Q **Can I do a check-up on myself?**

A Yes, you most certainly can - by looking at simple but important things like your weight, fitness level, and lifestyle habits. In some ways, you're the best person to do it, because you know more about yourself than any doctor or other health adviser could ever discover, and you're cheaper too.

So, in this chapter we'll look at simple ways of checking up on yourself and also some of the more important check-ups available from the professionals. Check-ups by alternative or complementary practitioners and therapists are covered in Chapter 7.

Q **Okay. Where shall we start? How about those bathroom scales you mentioned?**

A Good idea. Most people probably have this simple instrument at home, although the chances are that when you weigh yourself you're more concerned about your figure and your looks than your health.

'Perfect.'

Q **What exactly are the health risks of being overweight?**

A There are none if you're only slightly overweight. But once you start getting fat, your risk of various disorders increases: high blood pressure, diabetes, heart disease, gallstones, back pain, osteoarthritis of the hips and knees, and foot problems, to name but a few.

Q **But, how do I know if I'm fat?**

A Use the chart below to see just how your weight compares with what it should be for someone of your height. The chart applies to either sex, but remember, the categories are based on health risk, not on the way you look or feel about yourself. So you'll probably find that it's a little on the generous side. Remember too that if you have a wider than average frame (e.g. across the shoulders, or from hip bone to hip bone), or if you're particularly muscular, you can expect to weigh rather more without incurring any health penalties.

Q **What do the categories mean?**

A If you appear to be 'UNDERWEIGHT', you probably need to eat more of the healthy balance of foods outlined in Chapter 2. If dieting is ruling your life, or you're hooked on laxatives or slimming pills, or you deliberately bring food back up after meals, you have an eating disorder which may need medical attention. 'OKAY' means congratulations: you're the right weight for your height and your health. If you're 'OVERWEIGHT',

CHECK YOUR WEIGHT HERE

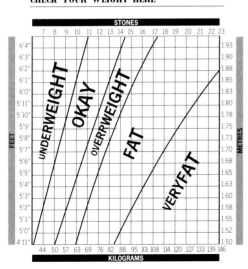

you need to slim – but there's no need to rush at it. No dieting is necessary: just change to a more healthy and natural balance of everyday eating (Chapter 2), and build up your physical activity a little (Chapter 4).

'FAT' means you have a real weight problem, and it's likely to affect your health if you don't get any slimmer. You must make every effort to cut down the fat and sugar in your food, and the alcohol in your drink. Follow the simple principles outlined in Chapter 3 and work out how you can cut your calorie intake by 500–750 a day.

'VERY FAT' means you urgently need to lose weight because it's almost certainly damaging your health. You've probably already sought the advice of your doctor. But if not, you really should – sooner rather than later. In the meantime, use the principles in Chapter 3 to help you cut your daily calorie intake by about 750 a day.

Q **That wasn't so bad. Now, how about my fitness level?**

A Right. This is a bit more complicated. Here's a quick quiz to start with:

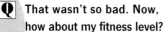

HOW TO TEST YOUR FITNESS

Q. DO YOU QUICKLY GET SHORT OF BREATH WALKING UPHILL OR EVEN ON THE FLAT?
A. *If yes, you really need to improve your stamina or staying power. Walking more is the best way to start.*

Q. DO YOUR LEGS ACHE OR FEEL WEAK AFTER A FEW FLIGHTS OF STAIRS?
A. *If yes, you need to build up your leg strength. A good way is to climb stairs more often.*

Q. DO YOU FIND IT DIFFICULT TO BEND DOWN TO TIE YOUR SHOELACES, OR PUT YOUR SOCKS OR TIGHTS ON?
A. *If yes, you need to improve your suppleness by daily stretching exercises and a more active way of life.*

Q. IS IT DIFFICULT TO REACH AWKWARD PLACES ON YOUR BODY, COMBING THE BACK OF YOUR HAIR FOR INSTANCE?
A. *If yes, you need to develop more suppleness in your shoulders. Again, stretching exercises are the answer.*

Q. DO YOU FIND IT DIFFICULT TO GET OUT OF A CAR, THE BATH OR YOUR ARMCHAIR?
A. *If yes, you need to improve the strength and suppleness in your legs and back.*

Q. CAN YOU WALK OR JOG FOR A MILE, COMFORTABLY?
A. *If yes, try timing yourself over a measured mile on the flat, without forcing it. Here's a rough guide to your stamina fitness rating.*

MINUTES TAKEN	FITNESS RATING
10 OR UNDER	VERY FIT
10-12	QUITE FIT
12-15	FAIR
15-20	RATHER UNFIT
20 OR OVER	VERY UNFIT

Based on averages for both sexes, aged 30 to 50. Younger people should be able to do better and should therefore grade themselves one rating lower. Older people should grade themselves one rating higher.

What about the bottom step of the stairs?

 Oh yes, nearly forgot. This is a simpler but less accurate way of measuring your stamina fitness. All you do is step up on to the bottom step and down again, repeatedly for three minutes, at a pace which is sufficient to make you no more than moderately breathless. Then you stop and, after 30 seconds, you measure your pulse rate (see box). Here is your stamina level:

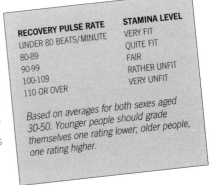

RECOVERY PULSE RATE	STAMINA LEVEL
UNDER 80 BEATS/MINUTE	VERY FIT
80-89	QUITE FIT
90-99	FAIR
100-109	RATHER UNFIT
110 OR OVER	VERY UNFIT

Based on averages for both sexes aged 30-50. Younger people should grade themselves one rating lower; older people, one rating higher.

 How can I check my pulse?

 The easiest way is to press in the groove on the front of your wrist, a few centimetres up from your thumb. Count the beat for 15 seconds and multiply the number of beats by four to get the total.

Stamina fitness is particularly important because it is achieved through regular aerobic activity, which, in turn, helps to protect against future heart disease.

 What other checks can I do on myself?

You can ask yourself about how your lifestyle may be affecting your health. Think about your eating habits and check to see whether they conform with the healthy eating principles outlines in Chapter 2. Putting on weight is only one consequence of an unbalanced diet. Too much fatty food can push up your blood cholesterol level (which we deal with on p.21) and too much salt can push up your blood pressure. Both of these are risk factors for heart disease or a stroke. And a lack of fibre in your food can lead to a string of disorders from constipation and piles to varicose veins and bowel cancer.

What about drinking?

 Yes, it might be important to check your drinking habits. And you can do this by totting up the number of 'units' of alcohol you consume in the course of a typical week.

One 'unit' of alcohol is equivalent to:

- *Half a pint of ordinary beer, lager or cider*
- *A pub glass of table wine*
- *A small pub measure of sherry, vermouth or port*
- *A single pub measure of gin, whisky, vodka or other spirit*

Remember, these are pub measures. Drinks poured out at home tend to be rather more generous!

There are clear guidelines from most national expert bodies on the limits for 'sensible' drinking. In Britain, for instance, the Royal College of Physicians, together with a number of other eminent organizations, has recommended the following as sensible limits:

- *For women: 14 units of alcohol a week*
- *For men: 21 units of alcohol a week*

 But that's nothing!

 Well, it does seem a bit Spartan, I agree. After all, many women would find just two glasses of wine a day a bit mean. And a lot of men would reckon half a pint of lager at lunchtime and a pint in the evening as virtually teetotal. But, for some people, any more than this and the risks begin to rise. See Chapter 6.

'*I guess it's not a great idea to have 'em all at once!*'

What are the sensible limits for smoking?

 There are no sensible limits for smoking. It isn't sensible to smoke any cigarettes at all. Even just a few a week will irritate your lungs and increase the amount of mucus your airtubes produce. The more you smoke, the more damage it does, and the longer you've smoked, the higher your risk of bronchitis, heart disease, lung cancer and cervical cancer.

Try breathing out through your wide open mouth as fast a you can: a huge and hurried huff. Was it a bit wheezy? That's your airtubes tightening up as a result of irritation. Try clearing your throat – ahem – as if you're unobtrusively trying to get the person in front of you in the queue to shuffle along a bit. Was the sound a little phlegmy? That's the mucus gathering. Do you find yourself coughing a lot when you first get up in the mornings? That's the beginnings of chronic bronchitis. Tips on how to give up are in Chapter 6.

 What other check-ups can I do on myself?

 Well, there are various ways of looking for early signs of disease. For instance, you can check your skin to make sure you haven't got a cancerous mole (malignant melanoma). See your doctor if you find a mole that shows any of the following changes:
- *it's itchy*
- *it's growing bigger*
- *it's blotchy*
- *its edge has become ragged*
- *it's inflamed, oozy or bleeds easily*

Always show your doctor any mole that's bigger than the blunt end of a pencil or has a mixture of black and brown areas within it.

 What else?

 If you're a woman, you can check your breasts every month (just after your period is best) for lumps and other unusual changes. Nine out of ten lumps found in this way are not cancer, but if you do find a lump or notice any other change in your breasts, you should get it checked by your doctor straight away.

HOW TO EXAMINE YOUR BREASTS

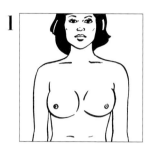

*Look at your breasts in the mirror as your arms hang loosely by your sides. Go through this **checklist**:*

Is the outline of the breasts normal? Is there any change in the size or shape or colour?

Are there any changes in the nipples? Is there any bleeding or discharge from the nipple?

Is there any unusual puckering or dimpling on the breast or nipple?

Are there any veins standing out in a way that's not usual for you?

*Now raise your arms above your head. Turn from side to side to see your breasts from different angles. Go through the **checklist** again.*

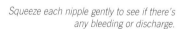

*Put your hands on your hips and press. Go through the **checklist** again.*

Squeeze each nipple gently to see if there's any bleeding or discharge.

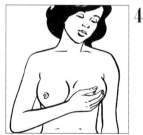

Now lie down on your bed with your head on a pillow. Put a folded towel under the shoulder blade of the side you are examining - this helps to flatten the breast tissue and make it easier to examine

Use your left hand to examine your right breast and vice versa. Put the hand you're not using on the pillow under your head.

As you examine your breast, keep the fingers of the hand together. Use the flat of the fingers, not the tips

And what about men?

 If you're a man, it's sensible to examine your testicles every month or so. Testicular cancer is much less common than breast cancer, but it's easily felt as an unusual heaviness or swelling. You'll need to get to know how your testicles feel normally, because they are meant to be a bit bobbly, especially on the top and at the back. One may also be a little larger than the other, and hang lower. But, if you feel something's different, or unusual, then don't hesitate to see your doctor. Testicular cancer is most common between the ages of 20 to 40 and in most cases, if detected early enough, is completely curable.

 What are the main check-ups available through my doctor or clinic?

 There are usually quite a few, particularly in the larger practices and health centres, but I can only deal briefly here with some of the main tests typically carried out as part of a well-person check-up.

Blood pressure

This simple test measures the pressure of the blood in one of the arteries in your arm.

The test provides two readings, such as 120/80. These numbers refer to the pressure of the pulse wave, both at its peak and its trough. High blood pressure usually doesn't cause any symptoms, but it must be treated effectively to make sure that the complications that go with it – a stroke, heart attack or kidney trouble – can be avoided. Everyone over 35 years old should have their BP measured at least once every three years.

Blood cholesterol

This is a blood test to measure the level of one of the fatty substances normally present in the blood.

High blood cholesterol is one of the main risk factors for heart disease. It leads to fatty deposits furring-up the coronary arteries, causing angina (chest pain) on effort, and, if a clot forms, a heart attack.

Most people in Britain have higher blood cholesterol levels than is best for them. This is probably due to the relatively high fat diet eaten in this country. If you're over 35, and you smoke, are overweight, or have high blood pressure, you should have your blood cholesterol checked at least every three years. Whatever your age, if you're immediately related to someone who developed heart disease under the age of 60, you should have your blood cholesterol checked at least every three years. High cholesterol tends to run in the family. For advice on cutting down on fat and lowering cholesterol, see Chapter 2.

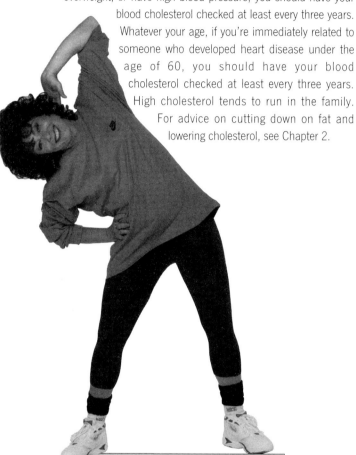

CHOLESTEROL: HOW HIGH IS TOO HIGH?

You'll be told your blood cholesterol level in the form of a decimal number. Here are the dividing lines:

UNDER 5.2	DESIRABLE
5.2 6.4	SLIGHTLY RAISED
6.5–7.8	HIGH
OVER 7.8	VERY HIGH

*'Good grief, you're right...
It does say Made in Taiwan!'*

Dental checks

Regular visits to the dentist are important in the fight against tooth decay (especially in children) and gum disease (especially in adults). In fact gum disease is thought to be the commonest of all diseases among adults, with about nine out of ten people over the age of 30 affected at least to some extent. Gum disease begins innocently enough, with a little blood when you brush your teeth. But, unless controlled, can eventually lead to loosening and loss of the teeth.

Eye tests

Regular sight testing is especially important for children and people over the age of 40. Young developing eyes need to be monitored to check whether glasses (or contact lenses) are needed. Older people's ability to focus on nearby things deteriorates in their 40s and reading glasses may be needed.

But eye tests are also a way of detecting various other disorders, particularly among older people. Diabetes may first reveal itself as an abnormality of the retina, the 'screen' inside the eye. So too may high blood pressure. Glaucoma is a disorder in which the pressure of fluid in the eyeball increases, damaging the retina. It's common among the over-50s and often linked to high blood pressure or diabetes. Cataracts, a clouding over of the lens, are very common in elderly people, but may also be detected and treated.

Cervical screening

This simple test – the cervical smear test – can not only detect cancer before it causes any symptoms, but it can also detect cells which might become cancer at some time in the future.

In Britain, all women aged 20-64, registered with a GP, are automatically invited to have a regular free smear test, and it may also be offered at family planning or postnatal clinics. Needless to say, the test is very worthwhile. It simply involves a brief internal examination and a gentle wipe of the cervix with a wooden or plastic spatula to pick up some mucus and cells. It may be uncomfortable, but it shouldn't be painful.

Looking at the cells under a microscope, the specialist can tell if they're 'dysplastic', which means that over a period of years they could become cancerous, though not necessarily.

If a patch of dysplasia is confirmed, it can be removed under local anaesthetic.

Breast screening

The screening test is a mammogram, a very low-dose X-ray of the breasts to detect a cancer at the earliest possible stage. Each breast is flattened gently against a special plate and the X-ray taken. Although this may be slightly uncomfortable, it's all over in seconds. In Britain, the NHS offers a three-yearly breast screening service to women aged between 50 and 64. An invitation is sent to all women in this age-group who are registered with a GP, and it's free. For women who are either under 50 or who are 65 or over, the service is available on request.

If you're in the age bracket for breast screening and you receive an invitation, make sure you accept. It's well worth doing for your peace of mind.

That's quite a long list.

Yes, but it's really just a very few examples. A full check-up could include urine tests, an ECG (heart monitor) and other blood tests. But the most important check-up of all is simply you telling your story. Your own and your family's medical history. And your lifestyle – exercise habits, stress level, smoking, drinking and, last but not least, your eating habits.

I'm hungry!

Okay. Let's tackle eating first.

66 *For God's sake it only goes in one little hole, why should it be such a big deal? Now they tell you what you stick in your mouth could be what kills you. So, of course, I go crazy. Meat – should I dump it or dice it? I don't want some heifer reducing my IQ points. Red wine – is it good for you or are you just too drunk to care? Who is this Polly Unsaturate and why can she clog up our hearts with chunks of lard? And then, is there someone in the phone book who can come over and suck it out again? Are they trying to make us insane? Now come on, they're just trying to confuse us, aren't they?"*

Well Ruby, I admit it certainly does seem like that sometimes. We do get bombarded in the media with an awful lot of conflicting advice. But you have to remember that there are big bucks in the food business. A lot of money rides on which foods are 'Okay' and which are not. And every week in the pages of our papers and magazines it seems one part of the industry is undermining another.

28 29

eat
WELL

31

So, how can we tell fact from fiction?

 Firstly by realizing that there's no such thing as a 'healthy' or 'unhealthy' food. What's important is the overall balance of different types of nutrients in our diet – fats, carbohydrates, proteins, vitamins, minerals – as well as fibre and water. One of the most crucial juggling acts is between the amount of fat we eat and the amount of fibre-rich complex carbohydrate (starchy food). Another is between the type of fat and the cocktail of vitamins.

Secondly, by recognizing that the 'official' advice on healthy eating from health education authorities with no particular axe to grind has been steady and unchanging for at least the last twenty years. The message is still essentially the same as it was in the mid-1970s: less fatty food, less sugary food, more fibre-rich starchy food, and plenty of fruit and vegetables.

 But what's so unhealthy about unhealthy eating?

 There's a long list of diseases and disorders that can be brought on by years, decades, of eating an unhealthy balance of foods. We touched on most of them in Chapter 1, but here's a reminder.

Coronary heart disease
Angina and heart attacks are mainly caused by the coronary arteries in the heart becoming silted up with a fatty substance called cholesterol. This is largely determined by our consumption of fatty foods, especially those high in saturated fats – mainly meat, sausages, pies, cooking fat and full-fat dairy products including butter.

Strokes
Damage to any of the arteries supplying blood to the brain is partly linked to cholesterol silting (as for heart disease), but even more importantly it can be traced to high blood pressure. This latter problem can be triggered by eating too much salt, drinking too much alcohol, or being overweight.

Diabetes

Diabetes in middle age is another problem that can be brought on by being overweight. It can lead to a number of complications, including cataracts and other eye troubles, circulatory problems, heart disease and kidney failure.

Bowel problems

Insufficient dietary fibre (mainly due to a lack of fibre-rich starchy foods, vegetables and fruit) is linked to constipation and a number of bowel diseases, such as piles, diverticular disease and bowel cancer.

Tooth decay and gum disease

Eating or drinking too many sugary things encourages mouth bacteria (plaque) to produce acid, which can destroy tooth enamel and inflame the gums.

Overweight

Apart from increasing the risk of heart disease, strokes and diabetes, an excess of body-fat is likely to aggravate such conditions as backache, arthritis, foot problems, and gallstones. It also increases the risk of post-operative complications. The most calorie-packed foods or drinks are those loaded with fat (or oil), sugar or alcohol.

Can all these problems be prevented by 'healthy' eating?

 Yes, prevented in the sense that the risk of getting them early in life can be reduced by eating a healthy balance of foods. Of course we've all got to die of something sometime, but by healthy eating we can help ourselves to fend these problems off until old age. In other words, healthy eating helps us to stay younger longer.

 So where are we going wrong?

 Just look at the typical British diet. High fat snacks, chocolate bars, deep-fried foods, fatty burgers, chips with everything, washed down with sugary drinks – the only concession to health is the occasional apple or banana.

HOW CAN WE CHANGE OUR DIET FOR THE BETTER?

Just remember this simple five-point plan:
- CUT DOWN ON FATTY THINGS
- CUT DOWN ON SUGARY THINGS
- CUT DOWN ON SALTY THINGS
- EAT MORE FIBRE-RICH STARCHY THINGS
- EAT LOTS MORE FRUIT AND VEG

Typical British diet

FATS

Q Why are fatty things so bad for us?

A Fatty foods in themselves aren't bad for us. Indeed some of the biochemical building blocks in fats, fatty acids, are necessary for good health. But eating too much fat, eating it too often, or eating the wrong sort of fat, is unhealthy in various ways. Firstly because of the link that has been found between a high fat diet and cholesterol silting up our arteries, particularly the coronary arteries (causing heart disease) and those supplying the brain (causing a stroke). And secondly, because fats of any sort are absolutely dripping with calories.

Q What sorts of fats are there?

A The word 'fat' makes most people think of cooking fat or lard and the fat on meat. But it also includes all those yellow spreads – butter, hard margarine, soft margarine, cream, full-fat milk and cheeses – many of which are loaded with fat.

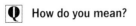

But don't forget that oils are fats too. They just happen to be a type of fat that's liquid at room temperature. Whether the oil is coconut oil or cod-liver oil, olive oil, sunflower oil or evening primrose oil – it's still fat. And it's just as fattening.

But from our heart's point of view, some sorts of fat are definitely 'better' than others.

Q How do you mean?

A Well, it all comes down to this business of 'saturated' versus 'unsaturated' fatty acids. These curious terms refer to their chemical structure and the details needn't concern us here – except to say that each type of fatty acid can have a different effect on our health.

Q Which are the 'bad' fats then?

A Saturated fats – fats high in saturated fatty acids. They're the ones mainly found in foods of animal origin – meat and meat products, milk, cream, butter, cheese and other dairy produce – but also in some plant oils, most notably palm oil, coconut oil and 'hardened' (hydrogenated) vegetable oils.

A diet high in these more saturated fats is likely to be linked to a high level of cholesterol in the blood, and hence silting of the arteries and heart disease. Most people should make a particular effort to cut down on these.

Q ...and the 'good' ones are unsaturated?

A Right. Fats or oils high in unsaturated fatty acids are kinder to your heart and circulation, and some even have a beneficial effect on your cholesterol level.

Q So, what are polyunsaturates then?

A Yes, well, this is where it starts getting complicated. Unsaturated fatty acids come in two main varieties: mono-unsaturated ('monos') and polyunsaturated ('polys'). Some unsaturated fats or oils are higher in monos than polys, while for others it's the other way round.

The polys are better known and broadly speaking, better for your heart. The richest sources are plant-seeds and fish – especially sunflower oil, safflower oil, soya oil, corn oil and fish oils. The polys in these oils not only have an anti-cholesterol effect, but also seem to make the blood less liable to thrombosis.

...and monos?

 These fatty acids are either neutral or moderately beneficial for your heart. Like polys, they're present to some extent in all fats and oils, but they're particularly abundant in olive, peanut (groundnut) and rapeseed oil. Chicken fat and fish oils have significant amounts too. Monos are thought to have a more modest anti-cholesterol effect than polys.

Needless to say, for your heart's sake, both monos and polys should be used to replace saturated fats whenever possible. One of the great benefits of the Mediterranean diet is its reliance on olive oil, fish and chicken.

 So, where's the fat in my food?

 It's a good idea to check the labels on packaged foods to see how much fat they contain, and what type of fat it is. Most products now list the fatty acid breakdown.

The most healthy fats of all are those from oily fish – which is probably why Eskimos have such a low heart disease rate. Sardines, tuna, mackerel, herring, pilchards and salmon are all rich in 'long-chain' polyunsaturates, which have a clot-reducing and anti-clogging effect on your coronary arteries. So, fish is good for your heart, even if it doesn't do a great deal for your brains!

As a rule of thumb, most of the fat in our diet is saturated and comes from meat and dairy products. Look for lower fat alternatives – leaner cuts of meat, chicken, white fish, low-fat sausages, semi-skimmed or skimmed milk, low-fat spreads, low-fat cheeses, low-fat dressings and sauces. Beware also the 'hidden fats' in chocolate, biscuits, cakes and pastries.

Choose oils and spreads 'high in polyunsaturates', and use them sparingly. When you prepare food, cut the visible fat off meat, grill rather than fry, and skim the excess fat off casseroles.

*'Poor thing, she's been on a prune and
high fibre diet all week.'*

FIBRE

 What exactly is fibre?

 It's basically what used to be called 'roughage' – although 'smoothage' would be a more appropriate term because it smoothes the passage of food waste through the digestive tract. This not only helps to prevent constipation, it also reduces the likelihood of piles, varicose veins, diverticular disease and bowel cancer.

 Yes, but what's it made of?

 Indigestible substances in fruit, vegetables, cereals, potatoes, beans, nuts and any other food from plants. Not just the stringy or pithy bits that you wouldn't want to eat anyway, but also softer substances in the edible parts.

Vegetarians eat about twice as much fibre as average meat-eaters and are much less prone to constipation or other bowel problems.

The greengrocer's shop or stall is a riot of colourful, flavoursome fibre-wrapped treats. There's lots at the baker's too, especially in wholemeal bread. And on the grocer's shelves amongst the brown rice and wholewheat pasta, the breakfast cereals, lentils and beans. But not at the butcher's or fishmonger's: there's no fibre worth mentioning in any food derived entirely from animals.

 Why is fibre so good for constipation?

 Because in the intestines it swells with digestive fluid, becoming a gelatinous mass which gives your bowels something to work on. About four out of ten people in Britain admit to being constipated, and about one in five takes laxatives. They would be much healthier (not to say better off) if they ate more fibre-rich foods instead.

Q But aren't these foods fattening?

A No, because the fibre itself is indigestible and not absorbed into the system. High-fibre foods are satisfying without being packed with calories. Indeed, they're often used as tummy fillers in slimming diets. Even fibre-rich starchy staples like wholemeal bread and potatoes are not particularly fattening because the starch is mixed in with plenty of bulky fibre.

Q So, is a vegetarian diet especially healthy?

A In a word, yes, it should be – as long as you take care to eat a variety of plant foods, with plenty of beans and grains to get good quality protein. Allowing some milk, cheese and eggs will help you get enough calcium, protein and vitamin D. Vegetarian eating is not only better for your bowels – it also helps to keep your cholesterol low, your blood sugar steadier and your weight down. And, of course, you can be sure of getting a healthy range of vitamins and minerals.

HOW MUCH FIBRE?

Approximate fibre composition of various foods

Wholemeal bread 8%	Bran flakes 12%	Sprouts 3%	Raisins 7%
Brown bread 5%	Muesli 9%	Cauliflower 2%	Bananas 3%
White bread 3%	Corn flakes 3%	Frozen peas 12%	Apples 2%
Almonds 14%	Rice crispies 1%	Baked beans 7%	Oranges 2%
Peanuts 8%	Carrots 3%	Canned sweetcorn 5%	
Bran cereal 28%	Jacket potatoes 3%	Dried apricots 24%	
Wheat bisks 13%	Spinach 6%	Raspberries 7%	

VITAMINS & MINERALS

 How important are vitamins?

 Very important. In fact they're vital – hence their name. Each vitamin has a different job, helping our body chemistry in various ways. They don't provide any raw materials or calories, so only small amounts are needed each day – for some vitamins, just a few thousandths of a gram. But they act as vital catalysts or biochemical lubricants, enabling various processes to happen, rather in the same way that only a few drops of oil are needed to keep a powerful engine running smoothly.

 What happens if you're missing out on vitamins?

 It depends entirely on which vitamin you're short of, and how short of it you are. A severe lack of each particular vitamin causes a distinctive disease, such as scurvy (lack of vitamin C), beriberi (lack of vitamin B1 – thiamine), or rickets (lack of vitamin D in children). Unfortunately, far too many people are eating so poorly that they may get some symptoms of vitamin deficiency, like excessive tiredness, lowered resistance to colds and easy bruising.

 Who needs extra vitamins?

Only those who are going short or who have extra demands made on them. Frail, elderly people living on their own might find shopping and cooking so difficult that they simply can't feed themselves properly. They are especially vulnerable to lack of vitamin C and the B group vitamins. Adolescents living on a very limited diet of crisps or biscuits and fizzy drinks might develop symptoms of mild thiamine (vitamin B1) deficiency. Slimmers who are avidly cutting fat from their diet may be missing out on the fat-soluble vitamins, A, D and E.

If you're trying for a baby, you're a special case. You should take extra folate (one of the B vitamins), in the correct dose advised by your pharmacist, until 12 weeks into the pregnancy. This helps to ensure your baby is getting all it needs and reduces the risk of various congenital problems.

People recovering from a debilitating illness or operation may need extra vitamins to help their bodies return to full strength. But if, like the great majority of people, you're eating a reasonably varied diet, you'll gain nothing from taking extra vitamin supplements. Your body extracts what it needs from your food and any surplus is excreted in the usual ways. All that you get for your money is very expensive urine!

*'Ah yes, a classic case of
calcium deficiency.'*

 Can megadoses of vitamins be dangerous?

 Yes, for some vitamins. Vitamin A, for example, is very toxic to the liver in large doses. There are also concerns that mega doses of vitamin C might lead to kidney stones. Another potential problem with large intakes of certain vitamins is that the body may have problems adjusting when the supplement is stopped.

 What about minerals?

 Yes, there are various minerals which are just as vital as vitamins. Iron, calcium, sodium, potassium, for instance, as well as magnesium, phosphorus, iodine, copper, and traces of others.

Iron is vital for healthy red blood cells. Although the body is very good at recycling iron, it's stores need regular topping-up otherwise anaemia could result. Women who have heavy periods or who are pregnant are especially vulnerable. Iron is present in a wide variety of foods, especially leafy greens, lean meat and liver (although this should be avoided if you are pregnant).

Calcium is not only crucial for bones and teeth, it also plays a part in the function of nerves and muscles. A plentiful supply is needed especially by growing children, pregnant or breastfeeding women and those on hormone replacement therapy. But the idea that extra calcium can prevent osteoporosis (weak bones) after the menopause has not been proven. Two-thirds of our calcium comes from dairy produce (including low-fat milks and cheeses) and nearly a quarter from calcium-fortified flour.

Sodium comes mainly from salt, and most people eat about ten times more than their body needs. For about one person in four, too much salt can lead to high blood pressure. We should all cut down on the amount we add in cooking and eating.

Don't overcook your veg, or most of the vitamins will end up in the cooking water. Use as little water as possible, and cook until just tender. Better still, use a steamer or microwave, or stir-fry in a very little oil.

Potassium is vital for every cell in your body. What's more, it has an anti-sodium effect and can therefore help to keep your blood pressure under control. Potassium is abundant in vegetables, potatoes, fruit (especially bananas) and juices. Yet another good reason for eating plenty of these foods.

To make sure that the foods you eat are as nutritious as possible, it's important that they are stored in a cool, dark place, so that they don't lose their nutrient value.

Frozen, chilled, dried or packaged foods can be as good a source of vitamins and minerals as 'fresh' foods. Frozen peas, for example, are easy to store, easy to cook, and highly nutritious, retaining their nutrients so well that they have more vitamins than fresh peas that have been sitting around too long.

ACE eating

There's increasing evidence that certain plant foods, particularly green and yellow vegetables, berries and citrus fruits, help to provide some protection against the development of cancers. These anti-cancer effects are thought to be due to the vitamins C, E and beta-carotene (vitamin A) which act as anti-oxidants neutralizing certain destructive waste products throughout the body.

 So, what exactly should we be eating?

 The basic healthy eating advice for people living in developed countries like Britain has been set down very clearly by the World Health Organization (WHO) and is supported by advice from our own Committee on Medical Aspects of Food Policy. These are the main recommendations of the WHO.

Eat much more fruit, vegetables and salads

We should each eat at least 400 grams (about a pound) of fruit, salads and vegetables (not including potatoes) a day. Tinned, frozen or fresh – they all count. This means *eating at least five portions* of these good things each and every day.

Eat much more bread, potatoes, cereals, rice, lentils or other starchy food

Because they are virtually fat-free, relatively low in calories and high in vitamins and minerals, fibre-rich starchy foods should form the basis of each meal, providing 50-70% of our total calories. This means the average person should double their present intake.

Go easy with meat, meat products, full-fat dairy products, eggs, cooking oils and other fatty foods

No more than 30% of our calories should come from fats or oils of any type, but not less than 15% for fear of missing out on essential fatty acids and fat-soluble vitamins. So the average person should cut their fat intake by between one-third and one-half. Foods high in saturated fat should be especially avoided.

Consider chicken, turkey and fish as alternatives

Poultry meat has less saturated fat than most red meat. Oily fish are fatty, but relatively low in saturated fats and high in beneficial polyunsaturates. White fish contain very little fat of any kind.

Eat sugary foods much less often

Refined sugar is a concentrated form of calories but has no other nutritional value. The WHO says we have no need whatsoever for refined sugar and recommends that no more than 10% of our calories should come from this source. For the average person, this means cutting sugar (in all its various guises) by about half.

Cut down on salt

The sodium in salt is essential, but we eat far too much of it. It's tasty and it's cheap, so manufacturers load it into all sorts of products. A high salt diet is thought to be an important cause of high blood pressure and strokes. The salt in bread, along with that naturally occurring in various foods, is quite enough for our needs. We should avoid salty foods and add less salt in the kitchen and at the table. The WHO recommends that our current intake should be at least halved.

'Ah fish again... quelle surprise!'

Q Isn't it all ever-so-slightly boring?

A Good grief no! Some of the most enticing and delicious cuisines in the world are also among the healthiest. Think of traditional Mediterranean food, for instance, with its emphasis on fresh, lightly cooked vegetables, or salads, together with bread, pasta or rice, abundant fish and a little meat, topped with aromatic herbs and rounded off with the freshest of fruits. Or the food of the Indian subcontinent, largely based on rice and vegetables, with its amazing range of exotic and scintillating spices. Or oriental food, again rice-based or with oodles of noodles plus lots of fresh vegetables (stir-fried very quickly to preserve vitamins), chicken, duck or, certainly in Japan, fish galore.

Q Well, it's too fiddly then!

A No, it doesn't have to be. Reaching for an apple, or opening a carton of low-fat yoghurt, isn't too troublesome. Cutting a thick slice of wholemeal bread or heating some baked beans needn't take too much effort. A healthy salad can be thrown together in a trice. Steaming fish or leafy vegetables takes not much longer. And if you have a freezer and microwave, you can make your own 'convenience' foods.

Q Surely it's bound to cost more?

A Wrong again. A healthy diet needn't break your budget. Vegetables and fruit in season are real bargains, especially from the market. Frozen foods may cost more than fresh, but are always available, with less waste. Staples like wholemeal bread, potatoes, cereals, wholegrain rice, yams and cassava are all relatively cheap. Steak is expensive, but chicken isn't. Salmon's a luxury, but tuna's good value. Instead of paying extra for carry-outs and pre-cooked microwave dinners, spend less money on a choice of healthy, wholesome foods.

What's the healthiest way to cook?

Any way which helps you follow the basic principles of cutting down on fat, sugar and salt, whilst retaining the natural vitamins, minerals and flavour of the food. Here are a few tips:

- *Whenever possible, eat fruit or vegetables raw or only lightly cooked. Wash them thoroughly to remove pesticide residues.*
- *Grill or bake rather than fry. Bake with foil to retain the flavour.*
- *If you need to fry, use unsaturated oil (such as sunflower, corn or olive oil), or dry-fry in a coated pan. Stir-frying in a wok is an excellent and fast way to cook small chunks of meat, fish, shellfish and vegetables in very little oil.*
- *If the children insist on chips, cut them thickly, parboil them and put them into very hot fat to seal them as quickly as possible.*
- *Skim the fat off casseroles and pot-roasts.*
- *Boiling, poaching and steaming are good low-fat ways of cooking, but use a minimum of water for a minimum of time to preserve vulnerable vitamins and minerals. Poaching or steaming is best for fish, especially white fish. Steaming leafy vegetables preserves their colour, flavour and crunchiness.*
- *Microwave cooking is fast enough to preserve much of the nutrient content and flavour. It's particularly good for potatoes, vegetables and fruit.*
- *Use less salt and more spices for seasoning.*
- *If you have a roast just once a week, forget about healthy eating and thoroughly enjoy it!*

But can I have snacks and treats?

Of course! Life isn't worth living without them. Some of the healthiest nibbles are also the nicest: apples, bananas, unsalted nuts and crunchy, salady things like celery, carrots, cherry tomatoes or sliced peppers. Dried fruit, raisins and dates are good too, and not too sweet. Low-sugar muesli or wholegrain cereal with semi-skimmed milk is a filling snack at any time of day.

Yes, but... you know what I mean... naughty wicked things.

Oh, well, if you really crave a cream-filled doughnut or a choccy biscuit... go on, have it. But just the one, mind! Or perhaps a couple. Only a very little of what you fancy; not the whole packet!

doughnut, biscuit, cake, chocolate, cream, cream, cream, cream, cream...

This is the big one. I reckon that for 99% of people – Okay, 99% of women – the whole 'health' thing is really about staying slim. All those salads. All that aerobics. It's all about being able to get into last year's jeans. There's got to be an easier answer. Surely some boffin will come up with a magic slimming pill soon.

Chapter 3

You can
be sure the drug
companies are falling over each
other trying to do just that, Ruby. The
potential worldwide sales would be
astronomical. But, so far at
least, the human body has
proved far too complex
to be that easily
fooled. True, there
are pills to suppress
your appetite, but they
make you jumpy. And pills
to speed up your metabolism,
but they make you even jumpier. So
it's back to the lab for the boffins – and
back to being careful about calories
for the millions who are
trying to lose weight or
stay slim.

Stay Slim

But why do so many people have a weight problem?

 There are a number of reasons. First, we're eating too many calorie-packed fatty and sugary things: too many deep-fried meals; too many high-cal snacks; too much chocolate.

Second, we're getting lazier. Our lifestyle is becoming more and more labour-saving and push-button. We now have effortless ways of doing almost everything. Not just the heavier jobs, but everyday activities like getting to work, washing clothes, mowing the lawn or sweeping the carpets and even tasks that take very little effort, like brushing our teeth or carving the joint.

More calories in, fewer calories used. Result: blubber!

 Why does fatness seem to be more of a female problem?

 Actually, in the strictly medical sense it isn't. More men than women are overweight and it has more of an effect on their health than it does on women's. Having said that, there are more very obese women than very obese men.

But you're right in the sense that women are more preoccupied about being overweight or oversize than men and go to greater lengths to do something about it. It obviously has a lot to do with wanting to look and feel good, and with current fashion. Only a minority of women say that health is the most important reason for losing weight or staying slim – whereas that's the main reason for most men.

 Are women naturally plumper?

 Yes. Women in the 'okay' or 'ideal' weight category (see the chart on p.14) have about 50% more body fat than men in similar categories. That's thanks to evolution: the extra fat not only gives women their characteristic curves but also provides them with a reserve energy supply that could, in times of famine, keep them alive and able to suckle their young. Men tend to be leaner and more muscular which, in evolutionary terms, makes them better hunters and defenders.

Q **But men don't do all that much hunting and defending these days. So why aren't they fatter?**

A Because muscle tissue burns up more calories than fatty tissue: not just when it's working, but even when it's doing nothing. So, men, generally the more muscular sex, burn up more calories than women whether they're mowing the lawn or slumped in front of the telly. It also means they can get away with eating more calories. Not fair is it?

No.

But, having said that, give them an inch, and they expand several. Far too many men are consuming far too much fatty food and alcohol. Hence all the pot bellies and spare tyres resting against pub bars and take-away counters.

Why do men put weight on mainly round their tums, whereas with women it's hips and thighs?

 Because that's the way we're made. It's a sex difference determined by our genes and hormones. Women are naturaliy pear-shaped – and plump women excessively so. Plump men, with their tubby tums, are more apple-shaped.

Apples and pears...

That's right. And these different body shapes carry different health risks. Studies have shown that the 'apple' form of obesity is more likely to lead to high blood pressure and diabetes. By contrast, the 'pear' shape seems to cause more wear and tear of the hips, knees and feet.

 What exactly is cellulite?

 It's a word coined to describe the dimpled plumpness of the hips, bottom and thighs that many women have. It's fat, just like any other body fat, but it's more under the control of the female hormones than fat elsewhere in the body (apart from the breasts). Although it can be reduced by dieting and exercising, it's maddeningly resistant. The fat cells in cellulite hang on to their precious contents long after other fat cells have given up, which is why many women are as skinny as a rake from the waist up, but fulsome in their hips and thighs – much to their chagrin. The unsightly dimpling characteristic of cellulite is due to the fat cells in 'cellulite' being bigger than elsewhere and bundled into large lobules of connective tissue attached to the skin.

So, what's the answer to cellulite?

 Unfortunately, despite the many claims you may read about in books and magazines, there's no specific way of tackling cellulite – unless you're prepared to contemplate having it surgically removed by liposuction. There are no special creams or potions to 'dissolve' the cellulite or break down the fat cells or connective tissue; no way of increasing the blood flow to 'flush away' the fat and unwanted metabolites; no special diet that targets hips and thighs; no exercises to remove the fat selectively from the offending areas. You just have to stay as slim as is sensible, by following the dietary guidelines in Chapter 2, and exercising to keep your bottom and leg muscles well toned-up.

 How come some people can stuff themselves silly and get away with it, whilst others only have to look at a chocolate biscuit and they put on half a stone?

 It's because we're all different, and we each inherit different body shapes different metabolisms, and different rates of ageing. Over the past few years, scientists have begun to unravel the mystery of how our bodies differ so widely in the way they cope with extra calories.

 And what have they found?

One important difference is the 'tickover' of our metabolism – our basal metabolic rate (BMR). This determines how fast we burn up calories when we're just doing nothing, in other words, the calories needed just to run our various bodily systems and processes whilst we're at rest. Yes, even reading about slimming burns up calories!

So how does all this affect how fat we are?

 People with a slow metabolism (low basal metabolic rate) tend to put on fat more easily. A faster metabolism burns it off and aids slimming.

 Can exercising speed up your metabolism?

 Apart from burning extra calories to power the actual physical work done, there's some evidence to suggest that it may be possible to increase the metabolic rate by exercising regularly. Some people have metabolisms that respond to daily vigorous aerobic exercise (such as brisk walking, running or swimming) by speeding up, not just during exercise, but for quite a while after it. Just think – if you're one of these fortunate souls – providing you exercise enough during the day, you can actually slim whilst you sleep!

Wow!

Yes, and another factor is the body's central heating system, called thermogenesis. This is a mechanism for dissipating excess calories in the form of heat. Naturally lean people are better at it than fat people – which explains their difference in weight. If a naturally thin person is fed a high-fat meal, their body responds by generating more heat, rather as if they switch on an extra bar of their internal electric fire. But a person who is prone to being overweight, even though he or she may be slim at the time, will respond to the meal by laying down fat straightaway.

 So people with a weight problem tend to put on weight more easily than people without a weight problem?

 Precisely.

 And their weight is bound to yo-yo up and down between diets?

 Quite. Well, one reason why 'going on a diet' is so often doomed to failure is that too many diets are just not real. They aren't proper eating. So, not surprisingly, when you come off them, you put the pounds straight back on again.

Another reason is that dieting leaves you hungry. Which in turn makes you miserable. Food becomes too much of a fixation: an emotional boost. At best this can tempt you to break the diet. At worst, it can lead to bingeing or even to the eating disorder bulimia.

The way to avoid all this is not to 'diet', but instead to change to a healthier, more natural balance of eating. Also you should try making physical activity much more part of day-to-day living, rather than an occasional blitz when you feel particularly bulbous.

Will it help me lose weight quickly?

 You know, this 'losing weight quickly' may sound wonderful, but it's not really a very sensible approach. You can lose up to half a stone within a week or two on a very low-calorie diet. But the weight you lose is not fat. It's mainly water.

 Did you say 'water'?

 Yes, plain old common-or-garden H_2O. It's released when your starving metabolism breaks down its emergency store of energy. That's not fat – it would take too long – but quick-release glycogen from the liver and muscles.

This happens in the first few days, and your weight drops steadily. Then suddenly... nothing! You've hit the famous slimmers' plateau. Your glycogen stores are depleted and the much slower business of breaking down body fat begins. Or doesn't.

 How do you mean 'Or doesn't'?

 Well, all too often, by the time your metabolism starts to burn up body fat, it has re-adjusted itself to cope with starvation. It adopts a 'siege economy', so that it doesn't actually need so many calories. And it slows right down.

This has two depressing consequences. Firstly, the plateau becomes harder to break through. And secondly, when you stop the crash diet, which sooner or later you have to, the calories are turned back into glycogen and body fat and your weight zooms up.

 You mean dieting can actually make you fat?

Yes, it can – if you overdo it.

Good grief! So what's the answer then?

 To take it slowly and steadily. To slim by stealth. Don't let your metabolism twig what you're up to. That way it won't need to re-adjust any of its settings. You can also step up your exercise, so that your metabolism is forced to burn calories – it has no choice.

'This diet's marvellous… I lost three pounds last week carrying it home from the supermarket.'

But it must take ages!

 Look, a staggering 95% of dieters fail because they try to lose too much weight too quickly. They either give up the struggle halfway through, or put the weight straight back on again as soon as they stop dieting. Yes, the sensible eating approach is slower – no more than a pound or two a week at most – but the weight stays off.

Strict, rigid, regimented diets may make you feel you're doing something definite and positive. It's easier to obey strict rules about exactly what you can eat and exactly when. But this only works up to a point and then it all-too-often collapses. And the reason why it collapses is that 'dieting' isn't natural and it isn't living.

Give yourself time. Use the progress chart opposite. Remember, a pound a week is nearly a stone within three months. If you want to look lithe and lissome on the beach, start changing your eating habits at least three months, and preferably six months, beforehand. Better still, start now for the holiday after next!

Don't be tempted to weigh yourself too often. Once a week is enough and try to do it at about the same time of day. Your weight naturally fluctuates perhaps two or three pounds (about a kilogram) during 24 hours, depending on how full your bladder and bowels are, when you last ate or drank, and even whether you've been standing up or lying down. Women should expect to be a little heavier in the days before each period, when their premenstrual hormones cause fluid retention.

WEIGHT LOSS PROGRESS CHART

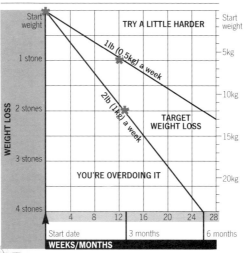

Mark your present weight with a cross on the left-hand side of the scale and put today's date (or whenever you want to start) at the left-hand end of the time-scale along the bottom. Assuming a weight loss of about 0.5kg (1lb) a week, mark a cross 6kg (about 1 stone) lighter in three months' time. Join the two crosses with a line. Now do the same thing assuming a weight loss of 1kg (2lb) a week, a total of 12kg (about 2 stones), and draw another line.

Weigh yourself weekly (not more often – it's demoralizing!) at about the same time of day and enter your weight on the chart. You should aim to keep your weekly progress within the two lines.

STODGE HELPS YOU SLIM!

Surprisingly, even when you're trying to lose weight, most of your calories should come from 'complex carbohydrates' – starchy staple foods – such well-known fillers as bread, potatoes, pasta and rice. Contrary to popular opinion, they're not particularly fattening. Instead, they fill your tummy with satisfying, low-calorie bulk.

Just don't smother them with lashings of butter or oil!

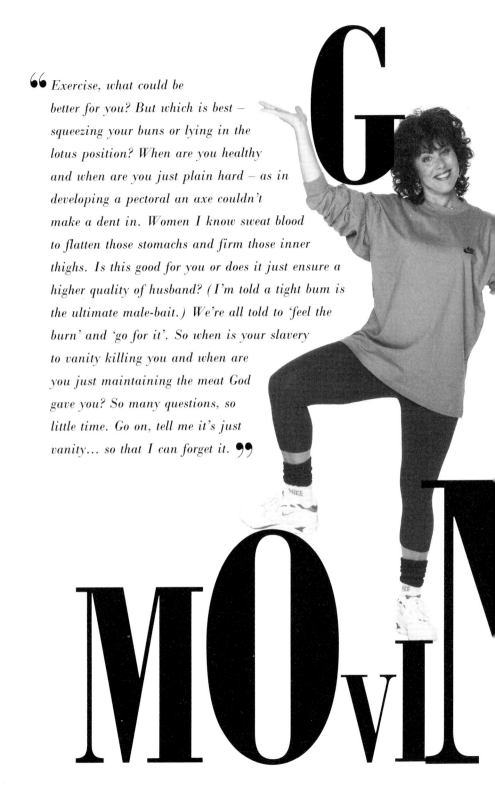

66 *Exercise, what could be better for you? But which is best – squeezing your buns or lying in the lotus position? When are you healthy and when are you just plain hard – as in developing a pectoral an axe couldn't make a dent in. Women I know sweat blood to flatten those stomachs and firm those inner thighs. Is this good for you or does it just ensure a higher quality of husband? (I'm told a tight bum is the ultimate male-bait.) We're all told to 'feel the burn' and 'go for it'. So when is your slavery to vanity killing you and when are you just maintaining the meat God gave you? So many questions, so little time. Go on, tell me it's just vanity... so that I can forget it.* 99

GOMOVI

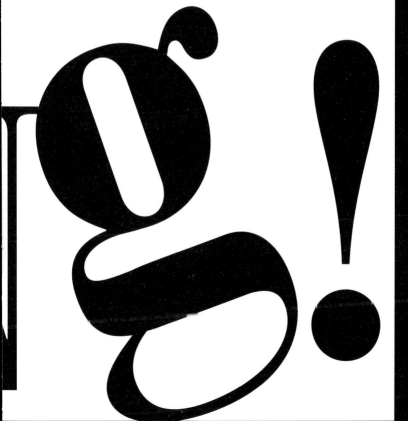

Well, there may be a bit of that in it for some people, but there's much more besides for everybody. More and more people are turning to exercise and an active lifestyle because it makes them feel good. More vibrant. More alive.

Are you serious? It's killing me.

A Okay, you may feel a bit tired while you're actually exerting yourself but, you must admit, you feel great when you stop.

 I do. I do! I must stop more often.

A Anyway you don't need to push yourself so hard when you exercise. It shouldn't be uncomfortable or unpleasant, and it most certainly shouldn't be painful. If it hurts, then you're doing something wrong. The old idea 'no pain, no gain' is a complete myth and a recipe for lots of pulled muscles and stiffness.

Q **But surely I have to work at it?**

A Yes, of course it takes some effort. After all, you want to burn up some calories and firm up your figure. But the point is that you don't need to punish yourself to do this. You just need to do a little more than you're used to, and very gradually build up your fitness.

> **STOP WHAT YOU'RE DOING IF YOU DEVELOP ANY OF THE FOLLOWING DURING VIGOROUS EXERCISE:**
> • *pain*
> • *dizziness*
> • *feeling sick or unwell*
> • *unusual fatigue.*
> *If the problem doesn't settle after resting, seek medical attention.*

Q So, what's so great about fitness? I don't want to be an athlete for goodness sake.

A No, and I respect your decision about that. But being fit doesn't have to mean being super-fit. It means being able to cope comfortably with the physical demands of your life. So, for ordinary mortals like you and me, it could mean having the stamina or staying power to be able to trot up the stairs or run for a bus without collapsing in a gasping heap. It could mean having the strength to lift your luggage or your child without straining yourself. It could mean having the suppleness to be able to nip in and out of the car, twist and turn, stretch and reach without seizing up.

Q Is that really why we're all doing it? For stamina, strength and suppleness? Is that what fitness is? Three 'S's?

A Well, yes. And I'd add one more. 'S' for Spring.

Q Spring? Spring who? What spring?

A Spring. Bounce. Zing. Pzazz. Attack. That extra oomph. That get-up-and-go factor...

*'I'm shattered already... and that was just
getting this rubber band on my wrist!'*

Okay, I'm getting up and going. You're telling me that all this hard work really makes you feel livelier? You're saying it doesn't wear you out – it actually energizes you? How come?

 Well, although you'll feel pleasantly tired immediately afterwards, the net result of taking regular exercise and becoming a generally more physically active person is that after a short while you'll begin to feel a lot more energetic, a lot more 'springy'. And here's why...

NEED A CHECK-UP?

Most people don't need a medical check-up before becoming more active or taking up some form of exercise. But if you have high blood pressure, a heart problem, chest trouble such as asthma or bronchitis, diabetes, arthritis or joint pains, severe back trouble, or you're recovering from an illness or operation, you should consult your doctor.

In fact, the right kind of activity is usually helpful for all these conditions, but, because it may have a bearing on your treatment, it's best if your doctor knows about it and can discuss the pros and cons with you.

Whatever activity you take up, always remember to start gently and build up gradually, day by day, week by week.

1. *Your muscles and circulation become toned up for action.*
2. *Exercise releases pent-up stress and lifts depression.*
3. *Physical activity stimulates the production of pleasure hormones in the brain. These morphine-like substances, called endorphins, make you feel good and give you a natural high.*

 You mean I could get hooked on exercise? I could mainline on the stuff?

 Well, after a while, regular exercisers often find that if for some reason they're prevented from taking exercise for a few days, they do begin to miss it. But certainly the feel-good factor is important and one of the main reasons why so many people get a lot of enjoyment out of being more active.

But what will exercise do for my health? I mean will I live longer – or will it just seem longer?

 Let's put it this way, research shows that regular exercise strengthens the heart, improves the efficiency of the circulation, helps to prevent high blood pressure, helps to keep your blood cholesterol in balance, helps to reduce obesity, and can cut the risk of coronary heart disease by up to a half. That's not bad for starters.

It's best not to exercise vigorously if you've got a cold, sore throat or a temperature, but wait until you feel better. You should also avoid vigorous exercise for at least an hour after a heavy meal – to let the food get down and prevent stomach cramp.

And, there's a major plus for women. If you have an active lifestyle, with plenty of exercise of various sorts, especially if it involves walking, running or jumping, you will develop much stronger bones, with a higher mineral density. You will be much less at risk of osteoporosis, the gradual weakening of bones that leads to so many broken hips and collapsed spines in later life.

 So, it helps you stay younger longer, right? Stand back, here I come! What other kinds of activity are good for all-round health and fitness?

 Lots of things. The choice is enormous. Broadly speaking, any activity is better than none, and if you do even a little more than you're used to, that's better still. The important principle is to make exercise part and parcel of your everyday existence, rather than a 'programme' that you have to force yourself into. So it's partly a matter of finding activities you enjoy, and getting into them with vim and vigour, and partly finding more physical ways of doing the things you usually do. Go for variety. The idea is to get a blend of activities that give you a good balance of those 'S' factors - stamina, strength, suppleness and spring.

Q Like marathon-running, caber-tossing, contortionism and bungee-jumping?

A You've hit on the most important consideration of all. Whatever you choose, it's got to be sensible and something you enjoy or at least feel really positive about. Because you've got to want to do it, to be motivated to keep active. It's not just for a few weeks to get in shape for summer, it's for life. So, going for walks, dancing, playing active games with the kids, fun things like that, are just as important as Exercise with a capital 'E'. The activities can change as time goes by. You can switch from step aerobics to swimming, or from badminton to golf. Do whatever takes your fancy at the time and fits in with your lifestyle.

'Yes, I think I've managed to fit regular exercise into my daily routine.'

So, how often should I do these things? And how hard should I go for it?

 Ideally, for stamina, slimming and a healthy heart, you should aim to have two or three sessions of fairly energetic activity every week, each session going on for about 20-30 minutes, getting you pleasantly breathless...

If you're pregnant there's usually no reason why you shouldn't keep up your favourite activities for at least the first six months or so. Exercise of some sort is positively beneficial throughout pregnancy as long as it's comfortable. But if you've suffered a miscarriage in a previous pregnancy, it's best to consult your doctor.

Steady on!

The sorts of activity that I mean are things like walking, aerobics, disco dancing, skipping, running, swimming, cycling, active games, or anything that gets you moving enough to raise your pulse rate and make you a little short of breath. The fact that you need more air means that you're burning up extra calories, your heart is working harder and your body machine is becoming better tuned and more efficient.

 What if I can't manage 20 minutes, two or three times a week?

 Well, a longer session just once a week would be good too. Especially if you do some shorter bursts for, say, five or 10 minutes on other days in the week. Again it's a matter of mixing and matching and fitting activity into your way of life. There are lots of opportunities, such as trotting upstairs instead of taking the lift, getting off the bus a stop or two earlier and walking the difference, spending more time chasing about with the children and letting the dog take you for longer walks. It's a matter of thinking more physical, and becoming a generally more active person in a whole lot of different ways.

Okay. Now how do I build up my strength?

 The stamina activities I've just been talking about are pretty good for your legs, but you may want to strengthen your arms, firm up your tummy or tone up your trunk, in which case you'll need to do exercises which focus on those parts. Using weights, for instance, or doing push-ups, will give you more strength in the upper half of your body and will firm up your chest muscles. As with stamina activities, two or three times a week is enough to make a real difference.

IF IT HURTS, YOU'RE DOING IT WRONG

Don't believe the person who tells you 'no pain, no gain'. This is a dangerous myth. Healthy exercise should be enjoyable, not uncomfortable. And certainly not painful. Never push yourself so hard that exercise becomes unpleasant.

 And suppleness?

You'll need to do activities or exercises that stretch you a bit and move your joints through their full range. If muscles aren't gently stretched they will shorten and stiffen. If this is allowed to happen to your neck or shoulder muscles, for instance, you'll have trouble reaching round to do up zips or brush your hair. If your back or legs get stiff, you'll struggle to get up from an easy chair or out of the car. Suppleness or flexibility exercises, for just a few minutes preferably every day, will gently stretch all your main muscle groups and keep you agile.

OUR DAILY HALF-DOZEN

ARM LOOSENERS

Keeping your arms straight, bring them together in front of you and raise them above your head, reaching back. Now separate them to each side, still reaching back, and bring them down again to your sides, and relax.

Repeat 10 times.

SIDE BENDERS

Feet slightly apart, arms at your sides. Slowly bend to the left and right alternately, allowing your hands to slide comfortably down the sides of your legs. Don't bend your knees or lean forwards and don't force it.

Repeat 10 times.

TRUNK TRIMMERS

Feet slightly apart, arms straight out in front of you. Fix your eyes on your right hand, swing it round as far as it will comfortably go, turning at the waist. Return it to the front and repeat with the left. Don't force it.

Repeat 10 times.

THIGH STRETCHERS

Sit on the floor, legs together, straight in front of you, knees flat. Place your hands on your thighs and gently slide them towards your ankles as far as is comfortable, stretching yourself forwards.

Repeat 10 times.

TUMMY FLATTENERS

Lie on your back on the floor, knees bent at right angles. Put your hands on your thighs. Now lift your head and shoulders off the floor and slide your hands towards your knees. Then let yourself down again slowly.

Repeat 10 times.

LEG TONERS

Stand with your feet together, arms at your sides. Bend your knees a little and spring up, landing with feet slightly apart. Now spring up again, landing feet together.

Repeat as a continuous movement 20 times.

So, I have a quick stretch every day, and do something a bit more demanding for maybe 20 or 30 minutes, two or three times a week – or less if I can't manage it – and I'm on my way to the perfect body and the picture of health. But wait. What about all the gear? I'll have to kit myself out properly, won't I?

 That depends on what you're doing and how stylish you want to look. You don't have to wear the latest designer leotards, or ultralite megabounce trainers. Most activities don't need a lot of special or expensive gear. Let's face it , you can go walking or running in almost anything. And if you're skipping in your own backyard you might as well dress down – who's going to notice? Of course, it's sensible to wear light loose cottons to absorb the sweat and let your skin breathe. And supportive underwear where you need it.

WARMING-UP AND COOLING-DOWN

For energetic activities, it's sensible to start with a few simple stretching exercises to 'warrm up' your muscles – particularly, calf stretches and hamstring stretches. These help to avoid sprains and strains. Similarly, after vigorous exercise, you can avoid stiffness by jogging loosely and then walking about a little.

 But once I've got myself really lithe and lissome, can I then relax, or do I have to keep it going for ever and ever?

 Once you really get into active living you'll want to keep it going for ever and ever, because it helps you feel good and it keeps you younger longer. So, yes you must keep it up to gain the benefits. If you stop being active, your fitness will soon melt away. The slide from being in great shape to a gasping heap takes a mere six weeks or so. You can't put fitness in the bank. But for each week that you stay active, not only will it be another week of feeling good and being in shape, but also another week in which the insidious processes leading to heart disease or osteoporosis are stopped in their tracks. So, think of it as holding back the sands of time.

Remember ...

**Exercise should be
a tonic, not a trial**
**It should be frequent
and it should be fun**
**The way to get
started is to just do it**
**Build up slowly
and gradually**
**Become more active
in everyday life**
**Check out your local
leisure centre**
**Keep it up: you can't
put fitness in the bank**

STRESS? WHAT STRESS.

66 Originally, when the caveman was attacked by a sabre-toothed tiger, a button inside him was pushed, a kind of turbo-engine, which gave him a little extra power for 'fight or flight'. Once the danger passed the button was released and things inside returned to normal. These days when faced with modern-day sabre-toothed tigers our buttons are still being pushed – at the office, at home, when we're driving and especially with builders or low-life plumbers. And because we aren't allowed to club these people over the head our buttons never, ever shut off. We become poisoned by our own 'fight or flight' juices. This causes stress. My question is how can we relieve ourselves of stress without ending up with a LIFE SENTENCE. 99

Actually there's quite a lot you can do.

As long as you really understand what stress is.

And how your mind and body react to it.

As long as you can recognize where stress is coming from.

And know how to handle it.

How to turn it to your advantage.

How to ride the tiger.

Some tiger!

Sure, the effects of stress can certainly be real enough to all of us. We feel tense. We get short-tempered. We grind our teeth, clench our fists, break into a cold sweat. Our heart pounds. Our blood pressure zooms. We start to shake. We may also become tongue-tied, over-emotional, forgetful: a bag of nerves.

 Is all that stuff healthy?

 Yes and no. It's certainly normal for us all to feel stressed from time to time. It's part of everyday life. For many people stress can be invigorating and exciting. They're the ones who work best under pressure. They get a high from stress.

But one person's stimulation is another's strain. If the pressure becomes a burden that gets on top of you, and you feel angry, trapped, inadequate or ground down, then that is strain. I sometimes wonder why we all go on so much about stress, when the real enemy is strain. Strain is what happens when we can't handle stress. And it's the strain we suffer that's the real enemy. It's the strain that can lead to so many health problems.

Q **What kind of problems?**

A Real physical symptoms like tension headaches, asthma, irritable bowels, skin rashes, indigestion, and conditions such as high blood pressure, peptic ulcers, colitis, heart attacks... the list goes on. Or habits that are likely to lead to problems sooner or later: eating disorders, workaholism, smoking, drink, drugs, gambling, partner-bashing. All of these are usually stress related.

Q **So, how can I cope with stress?**

A The first step is to recognize that stress is beginning to rule your life. This may not be obvious to you, but it usually is to those around you. Talk about it. Listen to what people are saying. Weigh it all up.

You may find that, by standing back for a moment and reappraising your life and the way you run it (or it runs you), you can make a few adjustments that pay big dividends in reducing stress.

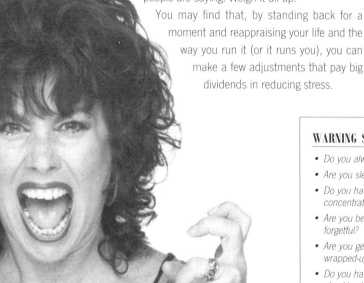

WARNING SIGNS

- *Do you always feel tired?*
- *Are you sleeping well?*
- *Do you have difficulty concentrating on things?*
- *Are you becoming more forgetful?*
- *Are you getting too wrapped-up in yourself?*
- *Do you have to keep checking things?*
- *Are you neglecting your family or friends?*
- *Does your patience snap more easily?*

Any of these could mean that stress is leading to strain.

But I have so many conflicting demands thrust on me.

I know the feeling. This is bound to be a real problem for anyone whose time is divided between family, job, friends or community. But you have to ask yourself which is really most important to you. Of course, they all are, but how much of your time do you devote to each? And how much should you devote to each? How can you re-adjust your life to get a more fulfilling and less stressful balance?

> **MANAGING YOUR TIME**
>
> - *Can you parcel out your tasks more efficiently?*
> - *Do you really need to do all the things you think you need to do?*
> - *Is there someone else who could take on some of your tasks?*
> - *Can you make some time for yourself?*

 But where do I start?

 If it all seems so overwhelming, you're probably trying to please all the people all of the time. This rarely works, and there's a real risk you'll end up pleasing nobody. So, grit your teeth – remember what's really deep-down important to you – and start saying no. It's tough, but you have to do this to stay afloat.

Next, divide those daunting challenges you're facing into smaller more do-able tasks. Instead of putting the whole thing off and pretending it can wait, tell yourself, for example, that, by the week after next, you will at least have made a start. And stick to it. Don't let it slide. Set yourself a series of short-term targets so that bit by bit you gradually get the job done or overcome the problem.

But my problems are huge and insurmountable.

Of course, you might have such major worries that there's no possible quick fix or easy answer. But usually, by carefully thinking through all the options, and talking them over with someone you feel at ease with, you'll find that solutions begin to present themselves, and that a way through the quagmire begins to emerge. It may not be ideal. It may not be without risk or drawbacks. But it is at least a course of action that you decide to take. And if you follow it through, and stick to your guns, without constantly looking over your shoulder, you could find that the stress miraculously diminishes.

Q **And what about all those everyday things that really wind me up? All the annoyances and frustrations that are guaranteed to make my blood boil?**

A Yes, we all have to live with these. Long queues at the check-out, constantly engaged phones, buses which refuse to appear, traffic snarl-ups, deadline panics, screaming kids, irritating in-laws, noisy neighbours, unreliable workmates... Just thinking about these stress-triggers is enough to give most people a headache. But imagine what the damage to your health could be over a period of years. The way you react to these situations is more important than you realize. All that pent-up anger, the clenched fists, grinding jaws and peaks of blood pressure: it all takes its toll.

BURBBURR

TWRRRILLL

Q Well, don't just pile on the agony. Come on, tell me. What can I do about it?

A Stress triggers will never go away, but recognizing them and learning how to cope with them is halfway to reducing their effects. Much will depend on how you bear the strain. You may be the type that doesn't want to know: you can't face it, you pretend it isn't happening, let things slide, head in the sand. Or perhaps you rush about faster and faster in ever-decreasing circles. Or maybe you explode. Or slump. Or just panic.

BURRRBURRR

'...and have a nice day, now!'

PANIC ATTACKS

A vortex of unbearable, unstoppable, sheer blind terror. At least one person in 30 suffers a panic attack at some time in their lives, many more women than men. But once experienced, never forgotten. Pounding heart, cold sweat, spinning head, fighting for breath – a dreadful experience.

Attacks usually happen in a crowded place – a supermarket, bus queue, a gathering – often triggered by a feeling of being trapped, or embarrassed.

They tend to be linked to an underlying anxiety or stress perhaps due to the premenstrual syndrome or menopause.

The best hope of conquering them is for the sufferer to recognize that the fear is coming from within, and not from the trigger situation itself – easier said than done. Family and friends can help by understanding the problem, and by helping the person to feel calm and unflustered.

But the only way to positively beat panic attacks is to learn how to confront the fear and see it off. This must be done in easy stages to gain confidence, and is best done with the help of a qualified psychotherapist.

PHOBIAS

Fear becomes a phobia when it's excessive and irrational, often leading to acute anxiety and panic. About one person in 10 has some sort of deep-seated fear or loathing that amounts to a phobia. But only a small proportion have it badly enough to seek help.

Phobias can be conquered only by facing the fear head on, instead of always running away from it. The most effective treatment is called desensitization and involves getting used to the feared object or situation in gradual step-by-step stages.

Whichever way you react, you'll need to make sure it doesn't add to your burden of stress, now or later. How you do this is the big question. Controlling your anger, irritation or anxiety can take a considerable effort of will. You have to tell yourself to stay calm and find some distraction or diversion, some way round the problem.

'I will not get stressed, I will not...'

Yes, yes, I'm waiting...

Well, for instance, when the traffic is making you tense, pop in a tape or do a few stretching exercises. When the phone is still engaged after your sixth attempt, or the bus sails on past your out-stretched arm, or the burning you can smell is the cake in the oven, don't hit the roof or kick the cat. Adopt a Zen attitude and recognize that these are all trivia. Try to see the funny side of it. Other people may fret and curse, but you can still smile. Whenever you find yourself in a particularly tense or frustrating situation, you can try these ways of using your body to relax your mind and vice versa.

Now you're talking.

The simplest of all is diaphragmatic breathing. Anxiety and tension make you take rapid, shallow breaths through your mouth, using the upper part of your chest. But by controlling your breathing so that you inhale slowly and deeply through your nose, using your diaphragm, you can ease away tension. Here's how.

Lie or sit comfortably, preferably in a quiet place, with your eyes shut. Start by taking in a very long, steady breath, right into every corner of your lungs. Hold it for a few seconds and then let it out very slowly without forcing any of it. Just relax, and let the air flow out under its own momentum.

With the next breath, don't deliberately breathe in, let it happen naturally, only as deeply as it wants to. Hold it – and relax. And the same again. And again. After a few breaths, you'll notice that your chest is doing less and less of the work and your tummy more and more. Eventually, with each breath, your tummy bulges slightly, and your chest doesn't move at all. This is diaphragmatic breathing, and it's very relaxing. Try to make each breath deeper, still only using your diaphragm. Feel yourself calming down.

 Mmmm, nice. What else?

In the same way that it's possible to become tense and nervous just by imagining some awful threat, it's quite possible to calm yourself by imagining something soothing and tranquil.

Make yourself as comfortable as possible, shut your eyes, and try to imagine a scene that conjures up a feeling of serenity for you. Perhaps waves lapping on a sun-drenched beach, or a waterfall, or a place in the country with the sound of rustling leaves and birdsong. Imagine the whole scene in detail and imagine yourself there. Wallow in the scene for as long as you can spare. Better still, do some diaphragmatic breathing at the same time.

Hey, I was well away there. Any other tension-busters?

Lots. Here's one that actually uses muscular tension to ease away mental tension. It involves first tensing, and then relaxing, groups of muscles, progressively from toes to head. It's a good one to add to your diaphragmatic breathing and serene thinking.

Again, lie or sit comfortably in a quiet place, and shut your eyes. Place your legs slightly apart and your arms a little away from your sides. Now, tense the muscles at the front of the calves, by pulling your toes up towards your face. But don't move your legs. Feel the tension for a few seconds, and then relax. Let the tension drain away. Now, do the same thing with the muscles at the front of your thighs by forcing your knees back and tightening your kneecaps. Feel the tension, and then relax. Let it drain away. Then tense your tummy muscles. Then your forearm muscles, by clenching your fists. Then your neck by hunching your shoulders. And finally screw your face into a tight wince, as if someone was about to pop a balloon right in front of your nose. And then relax. Just breathe deeply for a few minutes and let all the tension drain away.

I find meditation really works for me.

Yes, it's very effective. No-one should be put off by any preconceived ideas about flower-power, psychedelia or the lotus position. Meditation is a very simple technique you can use almost anywhere. It's been practised for centuries, especially in the Orient, and is a remarkably effective way of achieving inner calm. It takes diaphragmatic breathing, serene thoughts and progressive relaxation a stage further.

Lie or sit comfortably in a quiet place. Close your eyes. After a minute or so of deep breathing, and relaxing from the feet upwards, focus your mind's eye on a point between your two eyes, keeping them shut. Think of this point as a tunnel. Now let the tunnel draw you into it. Let it suck you in at an accelerating pace. Let it pull all your bodily tension through it into the far distance. Some people also hum a 'mmmmmm' sound with each slow breath out, but this isn't really necessary unless you're meditating in the traditional Buddhist way.

Don't worry if you can't imagine this to start with. It comes with a little practice. Once it starts to happen, you'll know the feeling. All your thoughts become focused into the tunnel, all distractions sucked in, and your head becomes wonderfully uncluttered.

After a few minutes of meditation, simply open your eyes and carry on doing whatever you were doing. You'll find you feel greatly refreshed.

And massage is *so* relaxing...

Absolutely. It's wonderful. It releases those knots of spasm in your muscles, stimulates your circulation, and... well, it just feels great.

The muscles most responsive to massage are those that are held rigid and static for most of the day, in particular, the muscles at the back of the head, neck, shoulders and down the back of the trunk. Massage of the feet is also wonderfully relaxing. Needless to say, you need someone else to do the massage for you.

Lie face down, preferably after a warm bath or shower, and preferably naked or nearly so. A few drops of an aromatic oil helps to smooth the action, and will also smell rather nice (see Aromatherapy on p.124).

There are many different techniques that can be used. Some involve firm, steady, kneading strokes with the flat of the hands, and some use deeper rotating movements with the heels of the hands or thumbs. Others employ the knuckles or fingertips, others rapid clapping or pounding movements. The important thing is not to touch too lightly because the slightest tickle will ruin everything.

YOGA

Yoga, in its simplest form, comprises a series of physical and mental exercises, postures or attitudes which relax the body and refresh the mind. The emphasis is on balance, muscle control and gentle stretching. The teaching usually also involves deep breathing and meditation. Classes are widely available and can be suitable for people of all ages and abilities.

Q **What other ways of relaxing are there?**

A An infinite number. Anything that gets you and your mind away from your worries. Rhythmic exercise is great for stress – skipping, running, dancing and swimming – but so too is soaking in a warm bath, listening to soft music, and having sex. Not necessarily all at the same time. A good night's sleep helps too.

'You know I feel really great already, no need to...'

SLEEP DRIFTING SLEEP

We spend about a third of our lives asleep. But, far from being a waste of time, sleeping is a vital function of the body. During sleep, most of the brain is simply ticking over and the neurones' chemical batteries are recharged. It's also a time when the body's resources do most of the tissue repair.

Despite this shut-down, parts of the brain are very active during certain periods of sleep. These periods, characterized by rapid eye movements under the closed lids, are called REM sleep. Dreaming is intense at these times, and it's been shown that people who are deprived of REM sleep, wake up irritable and unrefreshed. Too much alcohol or some types of sleeping tablets will reduce REM sleep, which accounts in part for the poor quality of relaxation gained from such sleep. A further sleep in the afternoon is often far more refreshing.

People need different amounts of sleep and often the quality is more important than the quantity. Older people do not need to sleep as long, but find 'cat-naps' through the day more refreshing.

Sleep well

About one person in 10 has difficulty sleeping, and it's one of the commonest reasons for seeing the GP. Difficulty getting off to sleep, disturbed nights, poor quality sleep, or early waking, are all forms of insomnia. The result is likely to be daytime drowsiness, tetchiness, strained relationships, poor performance, difficulty coping, aches and pains, depression, and an increased risk of accidents.

It's a problem suffered by only about 5% of under 30-year-olds, but as many as one in three of the over 65s, especially women.

POOR SLEEP PATTERNS

1. Try to find out why you're not sleeping well. Is it pain, discomfort, noise, worry?

2. See if you can deal with it in some simple way. Eat earlier in the evening. Have a warm bath. Give yourself an extra blanket.

3. Avoid caffeine-containing drinks, such as coffee and tea, in the two hours before bedtime. Try a warm milky drink instead.

4. Avoid spicy or stimulating foods late at night. Avoid cigarettes. And, whilst a little alcohol may help you sleep, don't drink too much.

5. Avoid vigorous exercise late at night, apart from sex. Intercourse is a great way to relax the mind and body.

6. Don't read scary books or watch exciting videos just before bed.

7. If insomnia is causing you real problems, see your doctor.

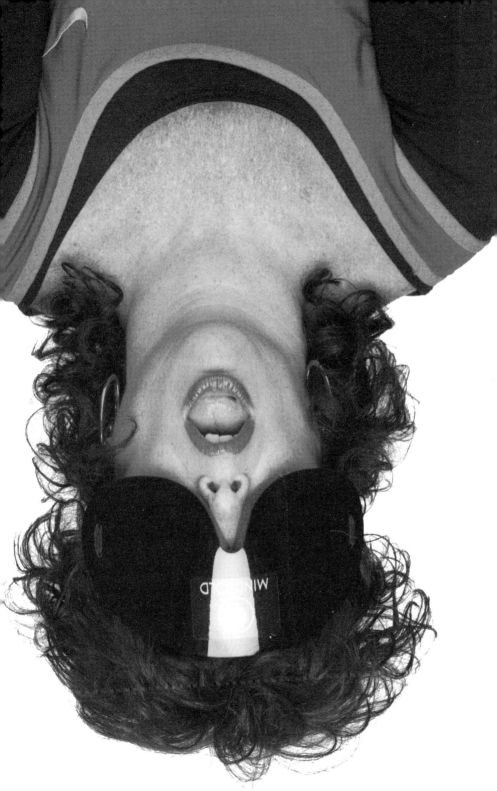

> 66 *How does it happen? I only wanted one cigarette. The next day my intelligent mind goes on holiday and is replaced by some sick reptile mentality saying, 'Go on, have 30 more, you'll stop tomorrow'. And of course tomorrow he makes me go out and kill for a packet. The real horror is, no one else sets the*

*un*HEALTHY *habits*

trap, only you. I've got a few bad habits, I don't mind telling you. Actually, I do mind telling you, and anyway I haven't really. Well, maybe just the odd little one, but I guess the odd little ones are usually the worst... 99

Well it's certainly a cruel trick that some of life's most pleasurable habits are often the most damaging. Over-fondness for chocolates, alcohol, cigarettes, or drugs, not to mention such familiar evils as promiscuity, gambling, reckless driving and too much TV.

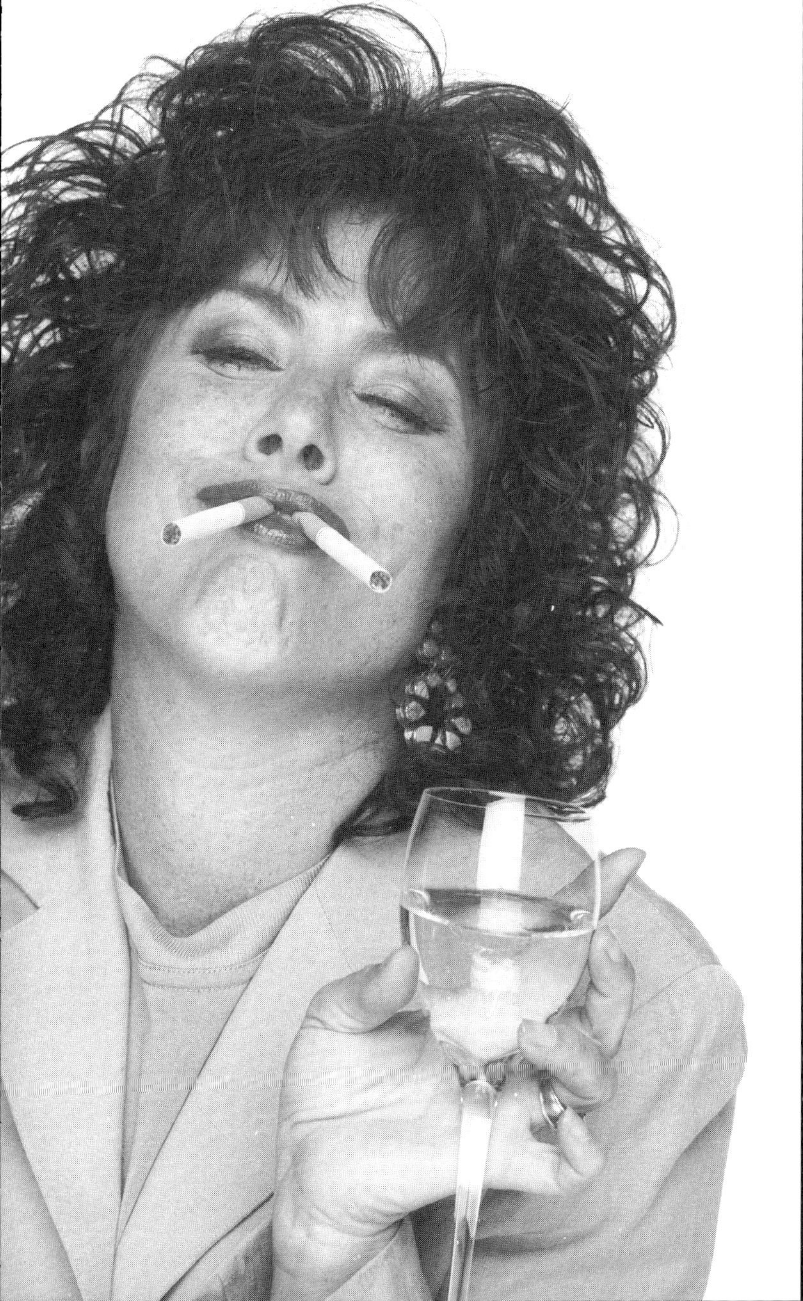

Chapter 6

SMOKING

 Too much TV?

 Yes. Soaps soften the brain. And they're almost as addictive as nicotine.

 How can smokers conquer the habit?

 The most important thing is to really want to. It's no good trying to give up if you're not completely convinced that you mean it, and you really do want to be a non-smoker. If you're only half-hearted about it, you're bound to fail. The road to wrecked lungs is paved with good intentions.

Okay, let's pretend I smoke, now convince me.

I couldn't do that. You'd have to convince yourself.

But there must be some facts and figures that would make me want to give up.

Well, maybe. But you probably already know that smoking increases your risk of heart disease, chronic bronchitis and lung cancer. You may not be aware, though, that it's also linked to many other diseases, including cancer of the cervix, bladder, throat and pancreas. It triggers peptic ulcers and worsens arterial disease, including that caused by diabetes.

But all that is light years away...

It may be a lot sooner than you think. Besides, if you're pregnant or trying to be, smoking increases the risk of miscarriage and the problems associated with a low birth-weight baby. And infants of parents who smoke are more likely to have chest troubles and glue ear.

Apart from all this, smoking pollutes the air people have to breathe, smells awful, is a fire hazard and costs an awful lot of money.

Right, I'm convinced. Now, how would I stop?

 The chances are that, if you were a smoker, you would have tried giving up before – perhaps more times than you care to remember. But the question is, were you really determined to succeed? Did you have enough encouragement and support? Did you follow a method, or just throw yourself into it?

Although nicotine is a strongly addictive drug, giving up needn't be as ghastly as you may think. If you're a smoker you'll know how long you can go without a cigarette. You'll know that it depends on what you're doing, who you're with and where you are. You may even have found that, in some circumstances, you can go all day without a cigarette and not miss it.

Much of the smoking habit is just that: a habit. You've got used to doing it at particular times of the day or in particular places: perhaps with your morning coffee, or whenever you're on the phone, or if you're waiting somewhere, or in the car, or at the pub, or at home watching TV... In other words, you find yourself in 'trigger situations' and – ping! – a bell rings in your subconscious and you reach for the fags.

So, to win at giving up smoking, you may have to overcome two hurdles, depending on what kind of a smoker you are. If nicotine is important to you, you'll have to shake off your physical and psychological dependence on it. And if you're locked into the ritual of smoking, you'll have to find ways of avoiding or breaking the triggers.

Yes but how would I actually *do* it?

 Here's a simple approach to giving up that covers both of these aspects and should suit nearly all smokers.

1. Make the decision and stick to it
This is the absolutely crucial first step. Unless you're convinced you want to be a non-smoker, and that this time you're really going to make sure you succeed, you won't stand a chance. Re-think all the reasons for giving up. Write them down, and put them in priority order. Think how much better things will be when you're a non-smoker. Not 'if', but 'when'. Try to persuade your friend, partner or workmate to give up with you – you can do a lot to help each other win through.

2. Prepare to stop
As with any battle, preparation is vital. Name a date to give up in a week or two's time – don't leave it any longer. It's no use saying you'll wait until the pressure's off a bit, it never will be. Pick as typical a day as possible.

Tell your friends and colleagues (especially the non-smokers) about your decision, and which day you'll be stopping. It will help reinforce your determination.

Cut down the number of cigarettes you smoke in the week beforehand. Miss out the less important ones. One trick is to put a rubber band round the packet so that you have to ask yourself each time: 'Do I really need this one right now?' Another trick is not to carry a lighter or any matches so that you have to keep asking for a light.

3. The day you stop

The moment you wake up, tell yourself you're now a non-smoker. You've done it. Make that mental leap. Convince yourself that, rather than being a smoker who's struggling to give up, you're a non-smoker who doesn't need to smoke and is not going to. Each time you get the urge to light up, don't give in to it. Refuse yourself each and every cigarette.

Aim to just get through this one day without a cigarette. Don't contemplate tomorrow, the next week or two, or the rest of your life. Just take one day at a time.

Remove all lighters, ashtrays and other smoking paraphernalia from your presence. Carefully avoid your smoking trigger situations. For example, have an orange juice instead of coffee, a sandwich in the park instead of a pub lunch, chew sugar-free gum when you're on the phone. Find diversions and distractions. If you find yourself in a tough spot and desperate, try deep breathing.

'So how's the no smoking campaign going then?'

4. Staying stopped

Follow the same principles as for yesterday. Take one day at a time. Find new ways of avoiding triggers: non-fattening things to chew or munch, things to do with your hands, fresh-tasting drinks instead of coffee or tea, new places to go in your breaks.

If you're worried about putting on weight, surround yourself with low-calorie comforters: mineral water, low-cal drinks, sugar-free gum, fruit.

Keep on your guard. It's very tempting after a week or two, or a few months, to tell yourself that you've cracked it and you can now have just one little ciggie as a reward. Oh woe! The classic error.

Tips for success

Heavier smokers should allow an extra three or four weeks cutting down before they give up completely.

Hypnosis or acupuncture can certainly help some people to give up smoking.

If you're particularly dependent on nicotine, try using nicotine gum, available from pharmacists without prescription. Nicotine skin patches are another method. They can double your chance of success.

Save the money you would have spent on cigarettes and give yourself a real treat.

How long will it take for the craving to stop?

A This varies. Some people find they are free from craving within a few days, for others it can take weeks.

 Could I not have just the occasional puff?

A The answer is an emphatic 'NO'. That's just treading the slippery slope back to smoking.

 Will I put on weight?

A Not necessarily, although some people do. Remember that weight gain after giving up smoking is usually temporary, perhaps lasting two or three weeks whilst the metabolism re-adjusts to the absence of nicotine. Then, as long as you're not consuming more calories, you should start to shed it again.

Q **How long will it take to recover from the harm of cigarettes?**

A A great deal depends upon what harm you have done already. You will immediately be free from the carbon monoxide and other poisons. Within days your breath will be fresher and your teeth cleaner. Your breathing and some circulation problems will resolve within weeks. The risk of heart disease reduces very quickly. That of lung cancer takes longer. But from the day you give up, your health prospects start to improve, and so do those of your young children.

It all sounds a bit daunting.

Sadly, some smokers, no matter how convinced they are about the dangers of smoking, and how much they say they want to give up, simply can't manage to kick the habit.

Yet thousands do succeed, despite these difficulties. And you can too. The stumbling block is all in the mind. If you've tried to give up, only to have failed miserably, don't worry, you're in good company. Just try again, but really go for it this time. Most people will make more than one attempt before eventually winning.

ALCOHOL

Another gin and panic please!

Steady on! Drink has its problems too. More and more women in particular are turning to the wine bottle for a little perk or comfort. OK, and even beneficial in moderation of course, but beware the slippery slope.

What a killjoy!

Yes, well, I'm only doing my job. A quick run-down of the potential problems. First, all the personal and social turmoil that can result: from accidents to arson, and from marital bust-ups to pub punch-ups. Then the diseases and disorders such as hepatitis (especially in women), cirrhosis of the liver, vitamin deficiency and loss of memory.

But you're talking about heavy drinking here.

Not necessarily. It doesn't take much to kill someone as you drive back from the pub or party. And steady tippling can soon turn a relationship sour. Even quite moderate drinking can increase the risk of high blood pressure. Just a few drinks each week can make the risk of problems for your unborn baby greater. And for slimmers the driest of wines is at least a hundred times as fattening as, say, a Diet Coke.

So, how much drink is safe?

 It depends. Shorter and less muscular people are more easily affected, so women tend to get tiddlier quicker than men. They're also more susceptible to liver damage. Alcohol is bad news if you're pregnant or trying to be. And of course, it's dangerous if you're driving or using dangerous equipment.

Having said that, as far as the long-term risks to health are concerned, there are clear guidelines from the Royal College of Physicians, together with a number of other eminent organizations. The current recommendations for 'sensible' drinking are to consume on average no more than:

- **14 units of alcohol a week if you're a woman**
- **21 units of alcohol a week if you're a man**

Above these limits, the risks begin to rise.

> ### WHAT'S A 'UNIT' OF ALCOHOL?
> - *Half a pint of ordinary beer, lager or cider*
> - *A pub glass of table wine*
> - *A small pub measure of sherry, vermouth or port*
> - *A single pub measure of gin, whisky, vodka or other spirit*
>
> *Remember these are pub measures. Drinks poured out at home tend to be rather more generous!*

'I think she may have a drink problem, Doc!'

How can someone deal with a drinking problem?

 The first thing is to recognize that it's happening, that drink is making life difficult, either for the drinker or other people. Perhaps the person drinks too much each time, or too often, or at the wrong time, or in the wrong place. Perhaps they're often late for work, or tired in the afternoons, or cantankerous with workmates or family.

Only a minority of problem drinkers develop a real physical need to drink, with real withdrawal symptoms if they go without. Most are psychologically dependent on the habit. They need to indulge in the ritual of drinking or the carefree mental state it produces, rather than to fend off the awful feeling of not having alcohol.

 How does problem drinking start?

 Imperceptibly. The important thing to realize is that there's no hard and fast dividing line between OK drinking and problem drinking. The one often merges into the other. Nor is there always a clear dependence on alcohol, some problem drinkers could give it up or cut down if they really wanted to.

Most people with a drinking problem either aren't aware of it, or refuse to admit to themselves that their drinking is beginning to get out of hand.

Q What are the warning signs?

A Again there are no definite rules, but plenty of clues that things aren't quite right. For example, does the person drink because they're bored, or unhappy, or stressed, or angry? Do they drink to feel better? More importantly, does the person look forward to their next drink? Are they drinking faster than their friends? Do they need a drink before important events? Do they switch to doubles for no real reason? Are other people noticing their drinking? Are they always the one to have a quick last drink? Are they spending too much on booze? Are they drinking more than they did a year ago? Or, as the habit gets more of a grip... Are they beginning to feel they may have a problem? Are they having trouble at work? Rows with family or friends? Are things not getting done? Bills not being paid? Are they drinking in the mornings? Do they have a secret supply of booze? Of course, most problem drinkers won't be showing all these signs. But if someone you know has a few of them, it may mean that they need help.

What can be done to help?

The first thing is to talk it over with the person as carefully and sensitively as you can. If you push too hard they may react by clamming up and denying the whole thing. Try and get them to open up about themselves – their hopes and fears, their joys and sorrows – over a drink if necessary. If they recognize that they have a drink problem, or at least might have the beginnings of one, then they may be prepared to seek some help, or accept it if it's offered. This might be from their doctor, priest or other trusted person, or perhaps from one of several organizations who can advise and guide people who have problems linked to drink. Confidential helplines are available for anonymous counselling. Or, for those who prefer to meet others with similar problems, there are local groups where drinkers can share ways of coping and conquering their need for alcohol.

HOW TO CUT THE BOOZE

1. If you think your drinking may be becoming too much of a habit, keep a diary of what you drink, when and why.
2. Try to find out what makes you want each drink. Is there some trigger you can avoid?
3. Cut down by switching to low-alcohol or no-alcohol drinks. Or dilute your drink with mineral water or another mixer to make it last. And sip rather than slurp!
4. Have alcohol-free days – at least twice a week.
5. Try to avoid drinking alone.
6. Find other ways to relax and enjoy yourself. A visit to the leisure centre, a walk in the park, an evening class – anything to keep away from drink and drinkers.

ANY GOOD NEWS?

Yes. Recent research suggests that your heart and arteries may actually benefit from a couple of drinks each day. Red wine is probably best, which may help to explain why heart disease is so much less likely among Mediterranean people. Unfortunately, the benefits are soon lost if you get to like it too much!

Cheers!

HOW MANY UNITS IN YOUR DRINK?

Beers and Lagers	*Units*
1 pint of Export beer	2.5
1 can of Export beer	2
1 pint of ordinary beer or lager	2
1 can of ordinary beer or lager	1.5
1 pint of strong ale or lager	4
1 can of strong ale or lager	3
1 pint of extra-strong beer or lager	5
1 can of extra-strong beer or lager	4

Cider	
1 pint of cider	3
1 pint of strong cider	4

Spirits	
1 standard single measure	1

Wine	
1 standard glass	1

Sherry, port, vermouth	
1 standard small measure	1

Low-alcohol drinks
Alcohol level varies but should be below 1.2%.

eg. 1 pint LA lager	0.6

Alcohol-free drinks
Virtually no alcohol present

eg. 1 glass of alcohol-free wine	0.0

DRUGS

The whole drug thing is getting worse isn't it?

 It certainly is. The use of illegal drugs is rocketing, together with all the problems that often come with them. But of course, there are drugs and drugs.

In a sense, we all take drugs of one form or another. Any substance that has a mood-altering effect can be considered a drug and many are addictive, either psychologically or physically. Apart from nicotine and alcohol, the caffeine in coffee, tea and cola drinks is a drug. And many prescribed medications such as sleeping tablets, antidepressants and tranquillizers are also drugs.

There's so much fear, ignorance and prejudice surrounding the whole question of drugs that people often forget that not all drugs are equally destructive, and not all people who 'take drugs' are evil.

Injecting anything has to be dangerous.

Sure, particularly if the needle or syringe is shared with another person. The risk of catching HIV, hepatitis B or other infections may be high. Then there are the dangers of the drug itself, such as respiratory arrest in the case of a narcotic like heroin.

 But what about other drugs?

 The easiest way to look at the problems is in the form of a chart.

A BRIEF GUIDE TO DRUGS

Solvents

- Inhaled as aerosol sprays, butane gas, glues, paint thinners, type-correcting fluids and even petrol
- Induces a few minutes of light-headed intoxication
- Can cause respiratory arrest and chronic lung damage
- Easily available to children

Cannabis

- Smoked as resin or 'grass'
- Causes relaxation, talkativeness and altered perception, of time, space, music and mood. Used medicinally for relief of severe chronic pain
- Little evidence of immediate harmful effects but the intoxication may cause accidents. Very heavy use may affect memory
- Not addictive. No evidence that it leads to so called 'hard drugs' such as heroin

Amphetamines

- Powder usually sniffed or injected
- Induces a state of alertness and heightened feeling of confidence
- Leads to exhaustion, confusion and paranoia if used continually. Higher doses needed each time. Can affect the rhythm of the heart with fatal consequences
- Most widely used stimulant, apart from tea and coffee

Cocaine and Crack

- Sniffed, smoked (crack) or injected
- Powerful stimulants similar to amphetamines
- All the problems of amphetamines plus nasal or respiratory disorders and chest pain. Higher doses needed each time
- Short-lived effects

Ecstasy

- Tablet taken by mouth
- Stimulant which increases energy with a heightened perception of colours and sounds
- Higher doses produce amphetamine-like problems. Deaths from cardiac arrest have occurred
- 'Rave scene' drug. Not addictive

Acid (LSD) and Magic Mushrooms

- *Taken by mouth*
- *Strongly psychedelic, altering perception, especially visual images and colours*
- *No physical side-effects, but bad trips are common and mental problems such as paranoia, nightmares and bizarre flashbacks can recur for months afterwards.*
- *Not addictive*

Heroin

- *Injected, sniffed or smoked*
- *Strongly psychedelic, altering perception, especially visual images and colours*
- *Strongly physically addictive. Very unpleasant withdrawal symptoms. A contaminated needle can cause septicaemia, thrombosis, gangrene, hepatitis or HIV/AIDS.*
- *Hugely expensive. Often leads to destitution or crime.*

 How can someone get help for a drug problem?

 Your GP will always give confidential advice and help, but you can also find specialist helplines, support organizations and clinics listed in the phone book.

BINGE-EATING

About one woman in four admits to frequent bouts of bingeing, chocoholism, stuffing themselves silly, call it what you like. Taken to extremes this over-indulgence in food can become the eating disorder, bulimia, involving mega-mega-binges followed by self-induced vomiting, excessive use of laxatives and very strict dieting. People with true bulimia (nearly always women, as with that other eating disorder, anorexia) aren't just over-conscious of their size and shape – it completely dominates their lives.

  How does it differ from anorexia?

Women with bulimia are usually of normal weight, except after a particularly heavy bout. Those with anorexia are always thin, often desperately so. Bulimia tends to first affect women in their 20s, anorexia in their teens. Anorexics also make themselves vomit and use laxatives, but almost complete avoidance of food is the big problem. Bulimia is more common than anorexia.

  Who gets it?

It tends to affect women who have problems with what psychologists call 'impulse control' (difficulty in resisting temptation), those with difficult emotional problems, such as an unhappy relationship, and those who have had anxieties or problems as children. There's a strong link with mood and hormones. Binges are usually more frenetic in the week before each period.

What do they eat?

 Sugary and fatty things. Chocolates are far and away favourites, but biscuits come a close second. Then crisps, cakes, you name it. Usually alone and secretively. Much guilt is involved. Afterwards there are tears, misery, and self-disgust.

 What help is there?

 The first thing is to recognize the problem. Binge-eating itself isn't a disease, but the consequences can be very distressing, particularly obesity and depression.

Ordinary dietary advice is usually not enough. Sufferers know perfectly well what they should and should not be eating. But talking it over with a trusted friend, or your doctor, can help. There are books on the subject to help you gain an insight into the problem. And advice is also available from self-help organizations and helplines. Some sufferers may need the help of a psychologist or psychiatrist. They may also be helped by acupuncture, hypnotherapy or other complementary approaches.

66 *A lot of my friends tell me not to take antibiotics because they'll eventually kill me. I thought they prevented that or am I very wrong? So they send me to some Chinese person who hands me twigs with instructions to boil them. Or better, they send me to a homoeopath who sells me a tab of belladonna. It's odd that we are so far along in civilization and yet we don't know if we're going backwards or forwards. I'll ask my astrologer.*

The trouble is that the conventional medical view of this whole alternative medicine thing is so excruciatingly BORING! No, it's worse than that. Doctors thrive on disease, it gives them power and a chance to indulge in all those dangerous drugs and high-tech tests. **99**

Well, believe it or not, the medical profession is at last beginning to see the value of at least some of the alternative or 'complementary' forms of health treatments.

Yes but most of these are about treating illnesses. Are there any that actually enhance positive health?

A Yes, I think this is their real strength. Quite a few can improve the balance between your mind and body and enhance your sense of well-being. In fact, most of them take a 'holistic' approach. Much of their strength lies in their attempt to see you as a whole person, with all your hopes, fears, lifestyle habits and relationships, rather than just another symptom or sick part. One of the great advantages of complementary methods is that the therapist or practitioner spends a great deal of time listening to you and really attempting to understand you. That's not always possible in the hurly-burly of medical care.

Let's take a closer look at the main alternatives.

Okay. Good idea. Let's start with A for Acupuncture.

An ancient Chinese healing art based on the notion that good health is dependent on the balanced function of the body's motivating energy, or Chi (pronounced 'chee'). According to the theory, Chi flows through every part of the body and is concentrated along channels beneath the skin called meridians. The circulation of Chi is governed by the two opposing positive and negative forces of Yin and Yang. If the balance between these two is upset – and this can be caused by a whole range of things – a state of disharmony will ensue.

 What's it used for?

 Pain – like migraine, period pains or backache. Lack of energy or disturbed sleep. Stress, anxiety, fear, anger or grief. Habit problems like over-eating, chocoholism, smoking, drinking, gambling and even compulsive shopping!

ACUPUNCTURE

Q What's involved?

A After taking a detailed history, the acupuncturist consults a chart of meridians and then inserts a number of very fine needles into the treatment points, so deftly you hardly feel them. The needles may be withdrawn immediatley, left in for 20–30 minutes, twizzled about a bit or electrically tingled with a tiny current and sometimes warmed with a smouldering herbal wick. A Japanese version uses finger pressure over the acupuncture points. This is called shiatsu or acupressure.

Q Does acupuncture work?

A Well, for one thing you should feel wonderfully relaxed once you've got used to the procedure. It can certainly be effective against pain – indeed it's used as an anaesthetic during surgical operations in China – and, unlike drugs, it doesn't have side-effects. No doubt suggestion plays some part; our threshold to pain depends a great deal on mood and attitude. Usually several weekly treatment sessions are needed to gain the full benefits, but the effects can last for up to six months or more.

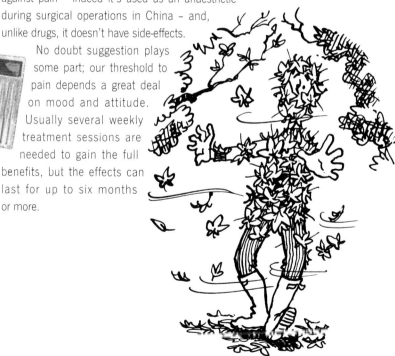

Never combine acupuncture with a walk in the country!

ALEXANDER TECHNIQUE

This is a system of teaching people how to balance their body in a directly mechanical way, which helps to avoid muscular tension and improve their poise, self-confidence and comfort.

It's a way of re-learning natural postures and ways of moving, rather than the artificial and distorting ones that most of us go through life with. It is taught by specially trained teachers who carefully observe someone standing, sitting, lying and moving about, and then show them what is wrong with their present movement patterns and posture, and how to put any problems right. Everyone can learn to avoid misalignment of his or her body and the imbalance of particular muscle groups and to improve their neuromuscular coordination.

I use Alexander technique all the time so I know it really works.

Yes, most people benefit from Alexander, because the chances are that their posture needs some sorting out. Anyone who has round shoulders, an angled neck or concave lower back can benefit from the technique. Musicians, singers, actors and dancers especially like Alexander because it helps them relax and control their movements instead of tensing up and ruining their performance.

NEUROMUSCULAR COORDINATION

AROMATHERAPY

Aromatherapy is a wonderfully relaxing form of massage using various aromatic oils derived from flowers, herbs, fruit and trees. But its devotees claim that (yes, you've guessed) there's much more to it than that. They say that it's an excellent way for the body to absorb the essences of therapeutic herbs, and that it can help to treat a wide variety of ills.

Q What does it involve?

A First, a careful note is taken of your physical and emotional needs, your symptoms and concerns. Then a combination of different quantities of oils is selected to match your particular requirements. The number of permutations is infinite, so the treatment is unique to you. Your skin is thoroughly cleansed before the oils are applied and massaged in.

'I calls it DIY aromatherapy.'

Q Does it work?

A Well, you'll certainly relax, and it's a marvellous, if rather expensive, way of moisturizing your skin all over. Certain aromas can evoke pleasant memories or sensations, and make you feel really vibrant. Unfortunately, there's no convincing scientific evidence that aromatherapy has any medicinal effect apart from loosening catarrh by breathing in the vapours. The oils are not absorbed into the bloodstream as some practitioners claim – and would probably kill you if they were!

Chiropractic is based on a form of manipulation related to osteopathy, developed by a Canadian, Dr Daniel Palmer, about 100 years ago.

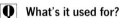 **What's it used for?**

 Low back pain, disc trouble, sciatica, neck and shoulder pain, headaches, hip and knee problems, pins and needles, and occasionally other maladies including arthritis, asthma, indigestion and arthritis.

 What's involved?

It's based on the principle that tiny misalignments of the spinal vertebrae cause an imbalance of the nervous system. The chiropractor takes a careful history and examines the person, paying particular attention to posture, muscle imbalances and tenderness. X-rays may be taken of the spine or joints.

Next comes the manipulation itself. This is aimed at correcting any misalignment or distortion, restoring mobility to the spine and joints, and removing any irritation of the nerves. Any stiff vertebrae or joints are gently unlocked using quick but comfortable thrusts or 'adjustments'. Several sessions are needed to achieve results.

Does it work?

It depends on the problem. Back trouble and neck pain usually respond well, and in many cases chiropractic can achieve better results than hospital treatment. Chiropractors certainly understand a great deal about the spine. Other conditions, such as arthritis, are less likely to be helped.

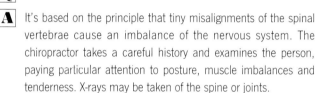
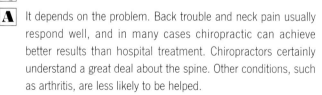

This somewhat intrusive form of therapy is certainly enjoying a vogue at the moment, and is very fashionable among the glitterati. It was first popularized at the spas of Germany and Czechoslovakia in the last century, but then fell into disrepute, before being revived again recently in New York, Los Angeles and London.

 What's it used for?

 The theory is that your energy and sense of well-being are dragged down by impurities and toxins gathered in your bowels. The more constipated you are, the worse this will be. But the therapists claim that even people with reasonably regular bowel movements may be harbouring these unhealthy substances. They say there's a long list of problems that can be helped by

*'I'm terribly sorry, but I think you'll find
colonial immigration in the building next door!'*

having 'a colonic'. These include halitosis, flatulence, headaches, allergies, tiredness, depression, ME, asthma and acne. What's more, some therapists see the treatment as a way of aiding slimming by removing the bacteria that break down food.

  What's involved?

It's basically an enema. You lie down on a couch and a nozzle attached to a clear plastic tube is inserted into your back passage. Measured volumes of warm water are alternately let in, and then drained out through another clear plastic tube. The tubes are clear so you can see the waste and bubbles being disposed of. All hermetically sealed. No smells.

The sensation, not surprisingly, is like that moment when, after an 'urgent call to stool' (as we doctors coyly put it), you've finally got there and can let it all go. Imagine that, repeated several times in a session lasting about 30 minutes.

  Does it work?

You'll certainly feel you've got rid of something – and if you're constipated that could be quite an achievement. But there's no medical evidence that it has any benefit whatsoever apart from giving you the feeling of having had a 'spring clean'. Eating a fibre-rich diet is a far healthier way of keeping your bowels moving. Nor will it decrease your absorption of calories. That all happens much further up your digestive system.

Orthodox bowel specialists say that colonic irrigation is not only utterly unnecessary, but also that it's potentially dangerous, with a risk of the bowel being punctured when the nozzle is inserted (although the irrigator would have to be pretty ham-fisted to do that). The idea that it's a way of curing ills and maintaining health, the orthodox experts say, is absolute piffle.

HERBAL MEDICINE

Thousands of plants have medicinal properties. Some British species even have popular names reflecting their remedial value: liverwort, heartsease, bloodstone, eyebright, spleenwort. The French call the dandelion 'pissenlit' (wet-the-bed) because of its diuretic properties.

Many of our modern medicines are based on herbal remedies. Digoxin, the life-saving heart drug, was developed from the leaves of the foxglove. Aspirin is based on an extract of meadowsweet and is related to another from willow-bark. Colchicine, a drug used for gout, came from the autumn crocus. Quinine, the anti-malaria drug, was extracted from the bark of the South American cinchona tree. Even antibiotics, perhaps the greatest step forward in orthodox medicine, originally came from moulds.

 What is it used for?

 Virtually the whole range of minor symptoms, from headaches to athlete's foot.

 Does it work?

 It depends on the ailment, and the skills of the therapist. Many minor conditions will respond to herbal treatments, although not necessarily any more quickly or completely than orthodox medication. Nor are herbal remedies as free of side-effects as many people believe. Because each extract or infusion contains a cocktail of substances, including the active ingredient, it may have all sorts of other effects on you as well as the one you're hoping for.

NATURAL ISN'T ALWAYS WHOLESOME

As most herbalists would be the first to point out, it's a mistake to assume that because the extracts, powders and infusions come from plants, and are therefore dubbed 'natural', that they're automatically good for you. Some substances from plants can be extremely toxic. Parents of young children are well aware how important it is to warn them about the many poisons in gardens and hedgerows. Most addictive drugs are extracted from plants: heroin from opium poppies, cocaine from coca leaves. And, let's face it, the biggest killer in the Western world, tobacco, is the dried leaf of an innocuous-looking plant, nicotiana.

HOMOEOPATHY

This is a form of 'medical' treatment which is intended to help the body heal itself by treating like with like. The substance prescribed induces symptoms and signs similar to those the patient is complaining of. This idea was first explored by the ancient Greek healer Hippocrates, using herbs and minerals. But the special system for preparing minute doses of such remedies was formulated by a German doctor, Samuel Hahnemann, about 200 years ago.

 What does it involve?

 As with most other forms of complementary medicine, you will first of all be interviewed in some depth about your state of health, your concerns, your family history, job, surroundings and so on. This is followed by a physical examination.

Then the homoeopath will match your profile with the appropriate treatment. The remedies used are prepared from repeatedly diluted extracts of plants and minerals. If you have no objection, animal extracts may also be used. This dilution of a dilution of a dilution goes on until the correct micro-dose or 'potency' is reached. Each dilution is thoroughly shaken or 'succussed'. Some potencies are so dilute that the active substance is barely present at all – perhaps just a few molecules.

 Does it work?

 Millions of people the world over receive homoeopathic treatment, and the great majority seem to derive real benefit from it. However, scientific appraisal of the treatment under controlled conditions has produced mixed results. Some trials come out in favour, others against.

There's one great thing in homoeopathy's favour though, you'll never suffer any side-effects.

So much of our awareness of pain and other ills depends on the degree to which our mind is 'bothered' by them. Hypnotherapy works by changing our subconscious attitude to a particular problem, be it pain, stress, compulsive eating or whatever.

 What's it used for?

 Pain, anxiety and compulsive habits like smoking, drinking and binge-eating.

 What's involved?

Well, for one thing it's not sleep. And, for another, you don't lose consciousness. Instead, it's an altered state of mind in which you let yourself, guided by the hypnotherapist, focus your thoughts into a concentrated awareness of some simple perception, perhaps the therapist's soothing voice, or a candle flame. This temporarily clears your mind of clutter and renders you much more receptive to suggestion. You become mentally prepared to accept what the therapist suggests to you. It's as though you allow the suggestion to reach into your subconscious, that mysterious part of your mind which governs your emotions and affects your attitude to so many things, including pain, illness, phobias and compulsive habits. In other words, hypnosis can enhance your will-power.

 Does it work?

There's no doubt that skilled hypnotherapists can help many people to cope with pain, and to kick such habits as smoking, compulsive eating and gambling. Surgery has been carried out under hypnosis. It has also been successful against phobias. But its effectiveness depends very much on how receptive you are to suggestion, and how confident you are in the therapist.

HYPNOTHERAPY

*'No there's definitely no term for someone who has a
morbid fear of hypnotherapists, Mrs Thompson!'*

Some of the basic ideas behind naturopathy are shared by
most other alternative therapies. Naturopaths maintain that the
whole patient must be treated, not just the disease or
troublesome part. The cause must be dealt with, not just the
symptoms. The real power of healing comes from within the
patient, rather than from some external agent. In other words,
the naturopath's aim is to mobilize the body's own life-force, to
potentiate the natural processes that fend off disease and
maintain health.

 What's it used for?

 A very wide range of illnesses.

 What's involved?

 Naturopaths are less concerned with the quick-fix of relieving
symptoms than with finding and dealing with the root cause.
Indeed they say that suppressing a symptom may drive it

deeper into the body. So the most important part of the naturopath's approach is to listen to your story, and find out as much about you and your lifestyle as possible. In other words, a very detailed history, including your dietary and other habits, your relationships, work, hopes and fears. You'll also have a thorough physical examination.

The essence of the therapy is to maximize the mind and body's potential through a combination of teaching – whole-food diet, fasting, posture, exercise, relaxation – and correcting mechanical misalignments by manipulation.

 Does it work?

 As with other alternative approaches to health, so much depends on your attitude to the ideas behind it and on your determination to make the changes to your life that will bring about benefits. The whole-food diet that naturopaths recommend is certainly healthy, being high-fibre and low fat, with lots of vitamin-rich fruit and veg. The fasting is, from a scientific point of view, quite unnecessary, but it isn't total starvation and won't do any harm. The emphasis on exercise, fresh air, good posture, and relaxation is all eminently sensible. The manipulation, along osteopathic lines, can help with many aches and pains. I see naturopathy as a useful complement to orthodox medicine rather than an alternative.

OSTEOPATHY

Osteopathy is a method of diagnosing and treating structural and mechanical problems of the body, using various forms of manipulation. It is closely related to chiropractic.

 What's it used for?

 The same sorts of aches and pains – backache, sciatica, neck pain, shoulder and arm pain, hip and knee troubles, headaches, sports injuries and so on, that is treated through chiropractic.

 What's involved?

 Osteopaths use conventional methods for diagnosing the source of trouble, including a careful history, full physical examination and, when necessary, X-rays. Up to this point, their approach differs little from that of an orthodox doctor. The main difference is their very thorough knowledge of the mechanics of bones, joints, muscle and connective tissue. Osteopaths spend about 60% of their time treating bad backs.

However, when it comes to treatment, the osteopath's methods are quite different. If they find a structural imbalance or misalignment (a 'lesion'), they use a form of manipulation that tends to be rather firmer and more forceful than the quick thrusts of chiropractic.

 Does it work?

 Well it certainly brings relief to a great many people – including lots who haven't been helped by conventional treatments. But not everybody responds, and even amongst those who do, it's often difficult to know whether the treatment has hastened recovery or whether it would have happened anyway.

RADIONICS

This form of alternative therapy is one of the most difficult to comprehend. In simple terms it's a form of divining or dowsing – along the lines of water divining – but using electromagnetic instruments instead of a twitching twig of willow or hazel.

 What's it used for?

 A wide range of minor physical problems.

 What's involved?

 In its most widely practised form, a hair or drop of blood from the person seeking help is used as a sample or 'witness' for their whole body. This sample is placed under the magnetic scanner of the radionic instrument, which is then tuned in to the person's 'energy field wave'. The practitioner mentally poses one question after another, not voicing them out loud, but conveying them through his or her own field wave 'in tune' with that of the sample. The patient doesn't even have to be present, although this procedure would normally follow a comprehensive consultation. By adjusting the magnetic scanner and reading various dials, the practitioner attempts to divine imbalances of particular organs or parts of the body. Various types of treatment are then given, usually herbal or homoeopathic.

 Does it work?

 Radionic practitioners claim that it has helped to diagnose thousands of illnesses where conventional medicine has failed to come up with the answer. But there's absolutely no scientific explanation for its apparent success, apart from the well-known powers of suggestion. Frankly, I think it's all mumbo-jumbo.

REFLEXOLOGY

This is an ancient form of foot massage first developed in China at about the same time as acupuncture, and based on the principle that the whole of the body is represented in a map on the sole of the foot. Different parts of the sole correspond to different organs. Sickness or disease of any particular organ is thought to cause 'crystals' or 'crusts' beneath the skin at the appropriate point on the sole. When these are massaged away by the reflexologist, the organ is stimulated and the balance of Yin and Yang restored. It has nothing to do with massage for tired feet.

 What's it used for?

 A wide range of illnesses, especially stress-related.

 What is involved?

 As with most other alternative therapies, you spend much of the first session talking about yourself – your symptoms, state of health, concerns, history and so on. Then you lie on the couch and the reflexologist carefully studies and examines your feet, before homing in on the part that needs massaging.

 Does it work?

 As with all these things, it depends on your particular malady and the skill of the reflexologist. Best results are obtained with migraines and other headaches, stomach pains, premenstrual syndrome, asthma, irritable bowel syndrome and various other stress-related states. There's no scientific explanation as to how reflexology might achieve results apart from a strong placebo effect: mind over matter.

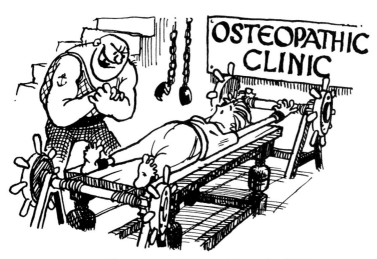

*'Now you wouldn't get this on the NHS
would you, Mrs Smith?'*

YOGA

Yoga (from the Sanskrit for 'oneness') is more a philosophy than an alternative therapy. But the techniques and attitudes learnt through yoga can be extremely beneficial to health. There are many different forms or disciplines of yoga, going back at least 2000 years, governing all aspects of life from mastery of the body (hatha yoga), love and devotion (bhakti yoga), service to others (karma yoga) and sexual fulfilment (layakriya yoga). Most yoga practised in the West is a simplified version of hatha yoga.

 What's involved?

 Control of one's posture, breathing, bodily functions and mind through a system of positions (asanas) and movements. The whole purpose is to refresh the mind and relax the body.

You gradually progress through these 'exercises', week by week, learning muscular control and balance, and becoming more and more supple.

Slow, deep breathing, using the diaphragm and abdominal muscles, is central to yoga, and has a powerful calming and harmonizing influence. Some yoga teachers advocate meditation – a wonderfully relaxing form of self-induced, mind-clearing hypnotic trance. They may also encourage you to change to a whole-food diet and submit yourself to periodic fasting.

 Does it work?

 Yes – there's no doubt it can benefit both mind and body. It's highly effective in relieving stress and tension, can reduce blood pressure, and improve the mobility of joints. A modified form of yoga can be especially useful during pregnancy, alleviating backache and teaching you techniques to help you cope with the birth.

Yoga classes are widely available in leisure and adult education centres, so learning how to do it is easy. Once you've grasped the essentials you can carry on at home in your own time.

ONENESS

Well, after all that, my well-being feels so enhanced I've forgotten what we were talking about.

You were questing for health Ruby. And we've covered most things now. I hope I've given you at least a flavour of how to go about getting the best out of life including the best of health.

Oh, you certainly have. Yes, indeed. But I've got just one more question...

Fire away.

What's the answer then?

How do you mean?

What's the Answer with a capital A? What's the ultimate secret of good health?

Good grief! What a question!

Well?

Well, if you really want to know, I think the 'Answer' is love. I think life is for loving and being loved. For helping each other to find happiness. I believe the real secret of good health is very simple. It's being as much in harmony with ourselves and our fellow creatures as we possibly can, whatever the state of our body. Health is harmony and harmony is love. All this advice about healthy eating and exercise and beating stress is all very well – it can help us stay younger longer and keep our body and soul together, and of course, it's very important – but without love, I believe it means precisely nothing.

Thanks. I'll go along with that.

INDEX

Acknowledgements

I'd like to thank Tony McAvoy of Prospect Pictures for bringing this challenging case to my attention, and Suzanne Webber and Deborah Taylor of BBC Books for their tender nursing care over many months. Thanks also to Dr Barry Lynch for a second opinion and Sister Jane for time and space at the convalescent home.

Last, but not least, we are all indebted to Ruby herself for being such an enthusiastic guinea pig and showing so vividly that good health is as much to do with irrepressible spirit and vibrant sense of humour as almost anything else. Thanks Ruby.